WHO RULES SANTA ROSA

AND WHY IT MATTERS

M. JAMES WILKINSON

iUniverse, Inc.
New York   Bloomington

Who Rules Santa Rosa and Why It Matters

iUniverse books may be ordered through booksellers or by contacting:

iUniverse
1663 Liberty Drive
Bloomington, IN 47403
www.iuniverse.com
1-800-Authors (1-800-288-4677)

Because of the dynamic nature of the Internet, any Web addresses or links contained in this book may have changed since publication and may no longer be valid.

ISBN: 978-1-4502-2532-8 (sc)
ISBN: 978-1-4502-2533-5 (ebk)

Printed in the United States of America

iUniverse rev. date: 4/23/2010

Dedicated to Ellen

for her exceptional forbearance and invaluable assistance

CONTENTS

CHAPTER 1

SANTA ROSA POLITICS AND ELECTION JIHADS

Jihads in Santa Rosa?? Sounds ridiculous, but in early 2008, a story circulated among civic activists that a local political power broker had privately said to a group of North Bay business colleagues, "Be very afraid – the progressive jihad is working to take away everything you hold dear." Whatever was actually said or not said, the existence of the anecdote reflected the fears of pro-developer political activists that their long-standing hold on the City Council might be in jeopardy at the ballot box in November 2008. They were right.

On the other side of the Santa Rosa political street, prominent progressives had in fact started early to raise funds and campaign for the 2008 elections. In the best traditions of American liberals, they proceeded as a loose coalition without the central direction and discipline that characterized the establishment's political machine. Nonetheless, they shared common goals, sensed the possibility of victory and worked hard to focus collective support on compatible candidates with the best chance of winning.

Underneath it all lurked two dissimilar visions of how best to guide Santa Rosa's path ahead. The one side – establishment political power – put its faith in the continuation of the development and growth that over the last half century powered Santa Rosa from a smallish provincial town to the center of regional commerce. The other side – disparate progressives – was increasingly concerned that the pattern of the past had to be changed with more care given to quality of life, natural resources and social justice.

When the dust settled after election day on November 4, 2008, progressives held a majority on the Santa Rosa City Council for the first time in history. The long reign of Santa Rosa's well-oiled "electoral machine" had come to an end, at least for the succeeding two years. The next few chapters of this book will take a closer look at the campaigns, personalities, and political dynamics that underlay this remarkable turn of events.

For the short term, the 2008 election result was something of a let-down. Despite the ideological changing of the guard, there was no money available to engineer grand policy shifts or new programs because the city was sinking ever deeper into a fiscal crisis. With the budget shrinking at the mercy of a nation-wide economic recession and a malfunctioning state government, the four Santa Rosa progressives who formed the new City Council majority sworn into office in December 2008 had to give full attention to the City's financial woes.

Still, fundamental political differences remain in play. Significant policy changes can be introduced that do not require significant budget expenditures, and, indeed, from the new Council's first weeks, numerous specific actions had to run the gauntlet of partisan contention. Looking ahead, new possibilities along with old contentions are sure to appear when recession clouds clear from the horizon – elections in 2010, 2012 and beyond will still be critical. How Santa Rosa shapes itself for a decade or more to come will hinge in large measure on whether the progressive coalition consolidates its gains or the pro-developer electoral machine finds the means to reclaim a council majority.

The parallel and far broader question for cities across America is whether the old ethic of maximizing growth can or should continue. Will prosperity be sustained by continued expansive development, hoping technological advances can mitigate the worst impacts of auto-dependency? Or do we need to think 'outside the box' to achieve more sustainable city development? Santa Rosa has already begun to ask itself what priorities should be followed to allocate limited city funds; how new projects should be assessed with regard to resource conservation and social justice; what should downtown look like; and how best to make neighborhoods less auto-dependent.

The two main factions in Santa Rosa politics have quite different answers to those questions.

THIS BOOK

This book explores the exceptional political ferment still bubbling in Santa Rosa, and what it all might mean for the city's future course. What are the motivations and dynamics behind the antagonism? Where does the colorful, if wildly inappropriate, notion of a "jihad" in Santa Rosa fit in? Who holds what so dear? Who is threatening whom? What is in fact at stake, what are the options, and how can our city best proceed to meet the challenges of the 21st century?

The chapters that follow pull together major political and economic developments, focusing on the last few years – in part to chronicle events, but more importantly to identify underlying trends and illuminate behind-the-scenes activities not obvious to the many citizens who have little time to follow these topics in detail. I hope the discussion will contribute to greater understanding of how this city's government works; promote government that is more open and responsive to community concerns; and encourage more participation by Santa Rosa citizens in making the decisions that will determine their city's future.

This is by no means an insider work that reveals any secrets. I will in places borrow private insights from influential personalities to

---

> ### SUSAN GORIN
> ### SANTA ROSA'S FIRST
> ### PROGRESSIVE MAYOR
>
> On December 9, 2008, Susan Gorin took office as Santa Rosa's first mayor from the city's progressive political tradition. She was elected to the City Council in November 2006. Her long record of community service includes a stint as a Santa Rosa Planning Commissioner, as well as membership, often as Chair, in many other organizations and agencies, among them, the League of Women Voters, Santa Rosa School Board, Santa Rosa Board of Public Utilities, and the Santa Rosa Bicycle and Pedestrian Advisory Committee.
>
> Gorin's declared areas of primary focus include planning for Santa Rosa's future, a sound economy, preservation of the area's natural resources, expanded public transit, safe roads for bicycles and pedestrians, and citizen participation in government. As Mayor, she has given high priority to overcoming factionalism on the Council – a daunting task given the persistent gulf between the hard-line pro-developer opponents on the Council and her own strong-willed progressive constituents.

3

shed light on a few shadowy corners or significant backstage happenings, but I have compiled the bulk of my information from public sources and interviews to describe the efforts of Santa Rosa's small army of political and civic activists – some better organized than others, and all passionate about their causes.

Nor is this book intended to rake up scandals or pursue insinuations of wrong-doing. I have no information or desire to go in that direction. At the same time, however, I will not shy from connecting the dots where there are appearances of *quid pro quo* activities, as for example, when like-minded people get together to support candidates for office and then work with officeholders to advance policies consistent with their group's priorities.

The parts and chapters of this book are organized on the following themes:

PART I - DESCRIBE AND ANALYZE SANTA ROSA POLITICS:

- *The political "seismic shift" from 2004 to 2008* (Chapters 2 and 3): Land development and pro-growth interests dominated the City Council from the end of World War II until the election of November 2008. How did it happen that the Council was transformed from a body controlled 6 to 1 by these entrenched forces in 2004 to one with a 4 to 3 progressive majority a scant four years later?

- *The Santa Rosa growth machine* (Chapters 4 and 5): A well-structured political machine emerged nearly two decades ago and skillfully managed to elect City Council majorities in a string of victories unbroken until 2008. Who is involved, what do they stand for, and how are they organized?

- *Santa Rosa progressive coalitions* (Chapters 6 and 7): A coalition of progressive candidates turned the tide in 2008. Who's who in progressive circles? What brought them together in 2008 with enough cohesion to beat the odds for the first time, and what are they doing to carry them through 2010 and beyond?

PART II - TAKE STOCK OF WHERE OUR FAIR CITY STANDS IN TODAY'S UNCERTAIN TIMES:

- *Crossroads, visions and plans* (Chapters 8 and 9): Santa Rosa's citizens sense that business as usual is no longer possible. The 'Great Recession' battered our economic landscape, and although recovery is underway as of 2010, things will not again be the same as they were before 2008. Where is Santa Rosa headed? How must the City revise its planning to cope with a projected population increase, budget shortfalls, demographic trends, and the overarching need for urban design tailored to the 21st century?

PART III - EXAMINE THE CHALLENGES OF SUSTAINABILITY:

- *Challenges and change to come* (Chapters 10 through 12): 'Sustainable' is the 21st century watchword, and cities across the country face urgent challenges in its three dimensions: environmental, economic and social. Virtually everyone agrees major new approaches must be found to "meet the needs of the present without compromising the ability of future generations to meet their own needs." What should such new departures look like, and how can the City set realistic goals, given that much depends on the national economy as well as Federal and State actions beyond the City Council's control?

CONCLUSION TO SUM UP THE POLITICS OF IT ALL:

- *Government Matters* (Chapter 13): The City Council has the ultimate authority and responsibility to chart Santa Rosa's course into the 21st Century, so it matters a great deal who gets elected to form a voting majority. What are the main points of contention and how would progressives differ from developer advocates in deciding the issues? And who is doing what to win elections in 2010, 2012 and beyond?

***

To set the stage for journeying into this complex territory, the rest of this first chapter will recap the current political backdrop and sort through local political labels that have all too often confused rather than illuminated the forces at work.

UNDERLYING CONSTANTS, CHANGE AND CHALLENGE

The underlying constants of tension in Santa Rosa politics are still issues of growth and development – what kind, where, and how much? Sustainability is now a key measuring stick, and it is proving difficult to master. It is fashionable to assert that Santa Rosa cannot continue with

SANTA ROSA -- SOME NUMBERS	
Population (2007 – est.)	158,000
Population (2000 census)	147,595
% white	71%
% Latino	19%
65 or older	14%
Elementary school students	
Latino (Oct. 2008)	52.5%
Mean household income	
(projection 2010)	$85,700
Below poverty line (2000)	8.5%
Homeless persons (2005)	1,160
Employment by industry (2000)	
Education/health	19%
Manufacturing	15%
Retail	12%
Population in 2035 projected	233,520

Sources: General Plan 2035; City School Dist.

business as usual, and there are many proposals for change. But talk is cheap, as the saying goes, and the hard part is forging a consensus strong enough to support action.

Santa Rosa's established community of developers and business allies still puts a great deal of faith in growth, looking for Santa Rosa to build up, as well as out, to fill in the Urban Growth Boundary. Progressives have a contrary perception, fast gaining credence, that the city's unrelenting pro-growth approach has run its course, and a paradigm shift is urgently needed to cope with the ever-increasing environmental and social pressures as well as to reverse the relative decline in the city's financial resources. The question of *sustainable* city growth will remain a dominant issue in Santa Rosa politics and is a central theme of this book. To one degree or another, the same issues are at the top of local government agendas all across America.

Santa Rosa's future character as well as its ultimate size will flow in large measure from the power of its City Council to control land use. For some developers and real estate investors, millions of dollars are riding on the outcome of Council deliberations, but profitable economic activity is of course only part of the picture – here as elsewhere, environmentalists, neighborhood residents and social justice advocates have other priorities and values – parks, open space, clean air, neighborhood character, preservation of heritage and protection of habitat. Pursuit of these objectives can clash with specific development projects or support constraints on growth in general.

Environmental issues have been important rallying themes for citizens in Sonoma County since the 1950s. In recent years 'greens' and environmentalists have been newly energized by the growing world-wide call for forceful action to combat global warming. The ranks of green activists have been joined by advocates for alternative transportation and cycling, better urban design, affordable housing, diversity and social justice. Later chapters will present some of the individuals who stepped forward in Santa Rosa to advance these causes, and directly or indirectly helped recast the city's political dynamic. Their activism and influence paved the way for the progressive victory at the ballot box in 2008.

In parallel with rising progressive activism, however, the 2008 political agenda had become enmeshed with the economic impacts of the nation's bursting housing bubble and the recession that followed. It was clear that Santa Rosa would have to take harsh measures to deal with serious budget deficits. When election time rolled around, the pressures on the city's financial position ballooned to a full-blown crisis, and continued revenue decline was clearly in the offing.

Although the recession began to break in late 2009, its full implications have yet to be divined for small cities like Santa Rosa. Experts differ on what comes next or what should be done to protect against another such debacle, but most agree recovery will be slow and the crisis was much more than just another periodic business cycle downturn. Santa Rosa will be hard pressed to sustain both economic activity and a reliable revenue stream for the city's budget. Progressives and developers split sharply on what needs to be done.

STEREOTYPES AND SPIN

Describing exactly where Santa Rosa's political fault line runs is no easy task. Conventional shorthand, used in newspaper stories and cocktail conversation, tends to promote a misleading stereotype that pits developers, often short-handed to "business," against "environmentalists." For example, the headline on a Press Democrat article in June 2007 read, "SR City Council's 2 Factions Lock Horns." The body of the article elaborated on the theme, noting: "The Council is generally split between two factions – one viewed as more business-oriented, the other more focused on the environment…"[1] Similarly, in 2000, a pre-election editorial in the same paper said, "you will hear plenty of huffing and puffing from business and environmental groups."[2] (The year 2000, it seems, was calmer days – "huffing and puffing" has to be less violent than a "jihad!")

Indeed, environmental concerns have been at the heart of some of the city's more contentious debates, involving such matters as Urban Growth Boundaries, the California tiger salamander, air quality, a bridge to take Highway 12 over Spring Lake, big box stores and ridge-top housing construction. And, as is often the case, when the 'green' ideal comes up against the cost of achieving it, perspectives can differ – implementing high principle may well mean lower return on investments.

But the stereotype of business people and environmentalists squared off against each other in Santa Rosa is at best ambiguous and often downright wrong. Most business people in Santa Rosa are good environmentalists – they have supported 'green' programs, notably those to

---

JOHN SAWYER
SR'S MOST RECENT GROWTH MACHINE MAYOR

In June 2008, John Sawyer was selected to replace the late Bob Blanchard as Mayor until the elections in November of that year. Sawyer was first elected to the City Council in 2004. A fourth generation Santa Rosan and owner of a downtown news store, he was by most lights the heir apparent to take over Blanchard's leadership of the pro-developer political machine.

Sawyer's public service record includes Chair of the Luther Burbank Home & Gardens Board, President of Santa Rosa Main Street and numerous other volunteer activities. His declared priorities have been public safety, a vital city center and improved traffic flow.

A staunch supporter of infill and most development projects (though he backed local business against a Lowe's big-box application), he also has gained attention for intemperate remarks, as when he lashed out at the Council majority which declined to reappoint him to a regional transportation board seat after the 2008 elections, and when he castigated the Mayor's leadership after Council selection of an interim City Manager in December 2009.

reduce greenhouse gases and promote efficient use of energy. In a similar vein, most environmentalists here want a healthy and vibrant economy – they are actively looking for ways to advance entrepreneurship and investment that takes advantage of green technologies and in the process contributes to business activity.

FOLLOWING THE MONEY

Where does political money come from? Examination of campaign funding presents a more nuanced picture than the foregoing stereotypes. Santa Rosa's premier political pundit, Mike McCoy, in a 2006 election piece,[3] identified Santa Rosa factions by "following the money." He examined City Council candidate campaign funding reports for the election campaign that year and found they divided into three groups:

--The first group (candidates Blanchard, Faber and Poulsen) in McCoy's analysis was funded in particular by construction interests and the investors behind a major residential project, Varenna, in the Fountaingrove area. McCoy called this "the business and development community."

--The second group (candidates Gorin and Banuelos, and "to a lesser extent, Jacobi and Taylor") McCoy identified was backed by "social advocacy, environmental, labor and neighborhood groups and their members."

--McCoy's third group of candidates comprised those "unaligned with either faction," and often heavily dependent on their own money.

It is noteworthy that the first group is relatively small, while the second is larger and considerably more diverse. McCoy's "business and development community" almost by definition has a readily identifiable common interest in continued city growth, but there is no single, comparably simple theme to hold his second collection of political associates together – social advocates, environmentalists, unionists, neighbors and their friends!

Santa Rosa's political make-up is not an isolated phenomenon. The same elements and patterns have been identified and analyzed in many academic studies aimed to better understand and describe America's special brand of urban politics. Variations of these economic and political forces come into play in virtually all American cities, all with underlying clashes of interests that run much deeper than summaries like McCoy's, which are necessarily abbreviated to fit news story constraints. Chapters 4 through 7 will look in more detail at the dynamics that drive Santa Rosa political competition.

GROWTH MACHINE AND PROGRESSIVE COALITION

I will use the phrase "growth machine" in this book to refer to the core organization that since the early 1990s has selected a slate of candidates, mobilized funding and managed campaigns for City Council seats. The terms "growth machine" and "pro-developer" machine or faction better match the political dynamics at work than words like "pro-business" or "business faction," since the central priority of past City Council majorities was the promotion of growth through large-scale development projects – led by the Santa Rosa Market Place and strip malls along Santa Rosa Avenue, the Fountaingrove and Skyhawk residential projects, and the more recent, unsuccessful, push for high-rise buildings downtown.

For political activists in the other corner of the Santa Rosa political boxing ring, I will use the term "progressive coalitions." As indicated above, the word "environmentalists" does not capture the complexity and breadth of interests that have been pursued in elections and led opposition to many of the Council's past pro-developer policies. Local environmental protection activists have regularly joined forces with advocates for bicycle facilities, historic preservation, affordable housing, diversity, homeless shelters and other community issues. Their collective political weight derives from a reliance on bases at the grassroots level and a perceived commonality of causes across a spectrum of generally liberal concerns.

Judging from my experience and contacts, the Santa Rosans who have regularly found themselves at odds with the growth machine are comfortable to be labeled "progressives." It is in the nature of their disparate issues and interests that they should come together through coalitions rather than under the leadership of a central political machine. At the same time, there are many in the city who would also label themselves progressive, but have not sought to play direct roles in City Council election campaigns – the Peace and Justice Center, for example, is one of several progressive organizations working on themes and activities that lie by and large outside the realm of municipal politics.

In any case, such shorthand references are bound to be problematic. Just because someone is not a declared member of a pro-developer faction, does not mean he or she is anti-development. And those who may not support environmentalist candidates are not necessarily anti-green. Real life is more complex than such summary labels suggest, and certainly so in Santa Rosa. My use of "growth machine" on the one hand and "progressive coalition" on the other is primarily an expedient, and readers should of course keep in mind that such brevity inevitably presents over-simplified pictures.

CHAPTER 2

SHAKING THE POLITICAL GROUND

In the 2004 general elections, the Santa Rosa growth machine slate swept to an overwhelming victory and set about with gusto to accelerate the city's development. Almost unnoticed at the time, however, the political ground had started moving in a different direction. Two years later, in 2006, progressives regrouped to win 2 out of 3 open seats, shaving the 6 to 1 pro-developer majority back to 5 to 2, and a few months after that, pro-growth stalwart Mike Martini resigned his seat to give full time to his private business.

Martini's resignation might not have changed much, except that Council Member Lee Pierce, rankling at his exclusion from the inner circles of the ruling faction, asserted his independence and broke ranks with the group. That led to a political "seismic shift" – the words of local columnist Chris Coursey – which upended the pro-developer establishment's absolute control of Council votes.

This chapter recaps events from 2004 through 2007. The changes shattered the growth machine's dominating position, and for a time created an evenly divided, sometimes unpredictable Council. Nonetheless, in comparison with previous years, this outcome was a progressive tilt that paved the way for the electoral victory of 2008 to complete the swing of power away from the growth machine. The next chapter will analyze the pivotal election in November of that year.

2004 – KINGS OF THE HILL

No one foresaw the coming dramatic shifts back when the political machine behind the majority on the Council was cruising into the new millennium. Following on a decade of continuous success, the pro-developer faction in 2000 held a 4 to 3 majority on the Council; in 2002, the machine increased its margin to 5 to 2; and in 2004, it gathered even more steam to take all four open seats and obtain a commanding 6 to 1 advantage.

Five of the six growth machine members on the Council after the 2004 elections came from the traditional Santa Rosa establishment mold: Mike Martini, founder of a winery business, had already served two Council terms, including a stint as Mayor; Janet Condren was also a two-term veteran and former Mayor; Jane Bender had been on the Council for one term and was re-elected in 2004 as incumbent Vice Mayor; newcomer Bob Blanchard was a former Deputy Sheriff and favorite of local public safety officials; and John Sawyer, also a newcomer to the Council, was a 4th Street news store owner who had been active in downtown business associations. The sixth was Lee Pierce, the first person of color ever elected to the City Council and a successful African-American businessman who had run a credible but losing campaign as an independent in 2002 before being recruited by the pro-developer machine.

With its 2004 victories in hand, the Council majority pressed ahead on ambitious plans for development of downtown Santa Rosa. It rewrote the zoning code and set its sights on realizing dreams of 12 and 14 story high-rises intended to transform Santa Rosa into something of a booming metropolis. "When can you turn the first shovel," asked Vice-Mayor Blanchard, brimming with enthusiasm at the Council's public hearing on approval of a Marin developer's proposal for a 14-story building, dubbed The Comstock, on 3rd St between Mendocino and D. And with the economy recovering from the bursting of the dotcom bubble, work proceeded apace on substantial residential construction in outer suburbs.

Still, there had been undercurrents of political change in the campaign of 2004. For one thing, the pro-developer forces for whatever reason did not rely on a slate of veterans from within their own tight circle, but recruited a relative outsider, Lee Pierce. to fill out their electoral ticket. In the process they repackaged his image and message – Pierce's 2002 campaign priorities with their progressive overtones – economic vitality, sustainable environment and social equality – were swapped out for new formulations more in tune with the growth machine slate – traffic, police and fire services and gang prevention through work with children. Pierce brought diversity to the ticket, but he was also a person who took pride in being his own man, with an independent streak that before long ran counter to the demands for conformity from growth machine leaders.

Some would add that the four-seat sweep of the pro-developer slate was more of a

VERONICA JACOBI
PROGRESSIVE CITY COUNCIL
MEMBER

Veronica Jacobi, elected to the City Council in 2006, is an engineer and small business owner. She is especially well-known as an active leader in organizations that champion the causes of environmental protection and conservation: the Sonoma County Conservation Council, the Sierra Club, the Sonoma County Water Coalition and the Sonoma County Bicycle Coalition.

On the City Council webpage, Jacobi lists her major areas of focus as safe, healthy and sustainable communities, climate protection, environmentally-responsible development and bicycle and pedestrian transportation. On the Council, she has typically been the first to assess environmental impacts of issues, but has also been a concerned advocate for local business, public safety and efficient government. Jacobi prides herself on being a listener and a promoter of citizen engagement – "one of the best ways to solve problems," she has said, "is for neighbors to sit down with neighbors."

progressive loss than a growth machine win. Progressives had in fact failed to fully exploit the potential of their disparate constituencies for the campaign of 2004. In the preceding elections of 2000 and 2002, they had been outspent and outperformed, and two of their strongest candidates, Susan Gorin and Marsha Vas Dupre declined to stand again in 2004, in part perhaps, a psychological consequence of their having been edged out when they ran in 2000 and 2002, respectively.

Nonetheless, in 2004 one progressive with outstanding environmentalist credentials, Veronica Jacobi, almost slipped into the winning top four. She lost by only about 500 votes out of 22,000, coming in fifth. Jacobi's showing was stronger than it might appear, since notwithstanding her substantial moral support from core environmental groups, she had otherwise campaigned largely on her own and was heavily dependent on her limited personal finances.

Below the surface of the campaign in 2004, two undercurrents of popular concern had begun to well up. The first, undoubtedly reflected in Jacobi's surprisingly good results, was growing recognition of the threat from climate change, a topic which had been rapidly moving up in public consciousness across the country. Interest continued to climb and before long was to get an enormous boost from former Vice President Al Gore and his film, *An Inconvenient Truth,* which premiered just after the New Year in 2006.

The other trend, specific to Santa Rosa, and largely unnoticed until the subsequent election campaign in 2006, was increasing voter disquiet over deep-pocket developer influence behind the growth machine's candidates. In 2002 progressive candidate Marsha Vas Dupre had called attention to the key funding role of a few wealthy developer and construction executives, only to find herself slapped down by the Press Democrat in a mean-spirited editorial for allegedly being "divisive."[4] The news pages of the paper had in fact reported objectively on the extent of developer campaign contributions in 2004, but the editorial staff found nothing untoward about the extensive role played by these special interests in Santa Rosa elections. On the contrary, Press Democrat editors in effect defended the outpouring of developer and builder money, and no progressive candidate followed in Dupre's footsteps to make it a major issue in 2004. In 2006, however, at least one poll found substantial voter discontent with the hefty role played by wealthy donors, and by 2008, all candidates recognized this change in public mood and took extra pains to rhetorically distance themselves from "special interests."

2006 – ELECTION TREMORS

In 2006, a significant course reversal set in at the ballot box. With three seats open, incumbent Vice-Mayor Bob Blanchard won reelection, but two other developer-supported candidates lost, breaking the impressive string of victories compiled in preceding years by local political campaign strategist Herb Williams. Susan Gorin and Veronica Jacobi, both backed by progressives, took first and third place respectively, shaving the pro-growth majority on the Council from 6 to 1 back to 5 to 2. By taking two of the three open seats, progressives gave themselves an important leg up for 2008, since they could gain a majority on the Council by winning only two of the four seats scheduled to be contested in that year.

Moreover, the numbers in the 2006 election, showed a marked tilt to the progressive side. Gorin whose campaign materials featured her backing from the Sierra Club, gained support on about 45%[5] of ballots cast for the Council, beating out Blanchard, who despite the benefit of incumbency, pulled in only around 36%. Third-place finisher Jacobi at 31% ran in large part on her record as a tireless advocate for environmental protection and succeeded in finishing well ahead of her much better funded growth machine opponents.

The issue of growth machine financing was brought to the fore in the 2006 campaign by an acrimonious brouhaha over an alleged "hit-piece" mailer. A progressive political action group, the Coalition for a Better Sonoma County (CBSC), sent out a postcard showing that two candidates, Shaun Faber and David Poulsen, had received the preponderance of their campaign funding from developer and construction interests. Both candidates reacted angrily to what they saw as an implication they were subject to undue influence, and Poulsen in particular mounted a vigorous counter-mailing effort with the

---

LEE PIERCE
FIRST PERSON OF COLOR TO WIN AN SR COUNCIL SEAT

During his four years on the City Council, Lee Pierce drew accolades for assuring passage of a tough outdoor anti-smoking ordinance, signing (as Vice Mayor) the Council's atypical resolution that called for consideration of impeaching President George W. Bush, and being the only Council Member to hold scheduled office hours for the public.

He took pride in being his own man and took pains to listen to popular opinion before casting his vote on key issues. These qualities in the circumstance of 2007/8 gave him the central role in changing the course of local politics to open up the doors of City Hall.

Pierce will be often cited as the first person of color to be a Council Member, and that has made him an important role-model for all minorities. Still, he himself always put more emphasis on his individuality. He lost his bid for re-election in 2008, in part because of a glitch that left a critical mailer unsent, but he has assured one and all that he remains an undeterred optimist and civic activist. As of early 2010, he was campaigning for the local area's open State Assembly seat.

vociferous support of pro-developer City Council members. In defense of the aggrieved pair, Mayor Jane Bender along with two political allies, former mayors Mike Martini and Janet Condren, signed a strongly-worded counter-letter (with a memorable typo in the title line that read "appology"). In the end, however, Poulsen and Faber finished well down the list (each receiving votes of only about 1 in 5 of all ballots cast), a result that confirmed electorate worries about just the kind of funding sources highlighted in the CBSC mailer.

After the election, the core pro-developer council members – Blanchard, Bender, Martini and Sawyer – wasted no time in trying to exploit what they saw as an opportunity to eliminate the $56,100 spending cap that applied to candidates in the 2006 election. They made the argument that candidates needed more money to be able to respond to "hit-pieces" like the CBSC mailer targeting Poulsen and Faber.

But Council Member Pierce was rankled by the sledgehammer tactics of his four colleagues in the face of clear citizen concerns. He broke ranks with the growth machine leaders for the first time publicly on an important Council action. "Pierce said the council must abide by the wishes of voters, who have said they want an end to big-money campaigns," reported the Press Democrat.[6]

Columnist Chris Coursey unleashed his trenchant wit against the action of the four pro-developer majority members, who muscled the resolution through the Council. He called the episode a "chillingly open display of power," in which the "big, buff political bully" crushed the "97-pound weakling" team of progressive opponents. Commenting on the strong-arm tactics of the majority, Coursey noted their self-interest in re-instituting their fund-raising advantage for coming elections. Echoing Pierce, he also castigated the majority for "sadly" ignoring public opinion, given that a dozen or more citizens showed up to speak for keeping the cap and not one came forward to argue for taking it off.[7]

Pierce's willingness to split from the growth machine on the vote proved to be a decisive turning point. His action as well as his declared reason for doing so, began to peel back the onion layers that had obscured the pro-developer majority's back-room *modus operandi* and its disregard for public opinion on issues important to its own survival or effectiveness. The dramatic climax came just a few months later.

2007 - THE "SEISMIC SHIFT"

"It may not have registered on anybody's Richter Scale, but a seismic shift occurred the other day on the Santa Rosa City Council ... when Vice Mayor Lee Pierce declared the ... group to be 'a 3-3 council,' sending eyebrows skyward throughout the council chambers." So wrote local columnist Chris Coursey in July 2007. "The ramifications," he added, " ... may steer the direction of the council -- and, by extension, the city -- through the 2008 election and beyond." [8] Coursey was right on the mark with this prophecy.

The ground under the Council lurched further when Mike Martini, a staunch growth advocate and pro-developer team player, resigned, saying he wanted to devote more attention to his private business. That would still have left the majority faction with a 4-2 controlling vote to pick his successor, except that Pierce, following his vote on campaign spending the previous December, had more and more asserted his independent bent. He continued to move further away from political consultant Herb Williams and the growth machine organization with which Pierce had associated himself for the election of 2004.

The split between Pierce and the pro-developer clique on the Council became open and irreversible with the vote on Martini's successor. As Coursey reported in his "seismic shift" column quoted above, "Pierce said after Thursday's council meeting that he has increasingly found himself on the outside of that group, including last week when Martini informed others in 'the Williams camp' in advance about his resignation but not Pierce. 'The Herb Williams camp has not embraced my style,' Pierce said."

Pierce's switch left the Council without a clear majority voting bloc on the question of a successor to Martini. Mayor Blanchard and his remaining political allies on the Council, Jane Bender and John Sawyer, had an obvious interest in picking a like-minded development supporter, but with Pierce on a different track, and Gorin and Jacobi in a different camp, the starting line-up divided 3-3 (or more accurately, perhaps 3-2-1). When initial votes were cast following an interview process, it became obvious that the successful candidate would have to be a political moderate, someone not committed for or against the long-ruling pro-growth majority.

A compromise was eventually struck by the two factions to avoid the expensive, and for that reason unpopular, option of a new election. On July 31, the Council appointed Carol Dean to serve out the 16 months left on Martini's term. Dean was best known as the leader of the West End neighborhood, who had mobilized residents to successfully rehabilitate the once-blighted area, organizing lawsuits and other actions to drive out criminal activity like drug dealing and prostitution. She had also served on the Board of Public Utilities and made a credible, if unsuccessful, election run for City Council in 2002.

> ### CAROL DEAN
> ### WEST END LEADER, POLITICAL DARK HORSE
>
> A legal assistant by profession, Carol Dean gained wide admiration for her successful work as President of the West End Neighborhood Association to clean up the residential area, save the historic DeTurk Round Barn, close down a drug house and get historic designation for the district. She also served with distinction on the Board of Public Utilities and the Charter Review Commission, and in 2002 ran unsuccessfully for City Council.
>
> Dean had always manifested an independent streak, but given her record of neighborhood activism, many were surprised after her appointment to fill the Council vacancy in 2007, when she drifted not into the progressive camp, but over to the growth machine side. In any case, voters did not, it seemed, take kindly to her withdrawal of a pledge not to run in 2008, and she finished well back when she ran for election to continue on the Council. In March 2008, she was appointed by the Governor Schwarzenegger to the prestigious North Coast Regional Water Quality Control Board.

Dean obviously held the pivotal vote to break the 3-3 split between the rest of her colleagues, and council watchers looked for hints of where she might come down on key votes. Her record showed what many would consider a generally cautious approach to development issues, but her experience had also made her leery of what she evidently found to be unreasonable progressive efforts to push bicycle facilities and affordable housing in or near her West End neighborhood.

PRE-ELECTION DEADLOCK

Before a new majority line-up emerged, however, Mayor Bob Blanchard tragically succumbed after a valiant three-year battle with cancer. Forced by the illness to resign in late May, he passed away on June 14, 2008, mourned by all who knew him as a high-spirited individual, vigorous community leader and enthusiastic booster of our fair city. With the 2008 election less than six months away, there was no perceived need to fill the vacancy, and it was left to voters to pick a replacement in general elections on November 4. Vice Mayor John Sawyer, a close friend and political associate of Blanchard's, was selected as Mayor to serve until the November ballot.

The pendulum of power on the remaining six-member Council by and large stayed in the middle. Dean had disagreed with progressives on the Council over the spending limit to be specified in the campaign finance reform ordinance – she wanted $30,000, while others favored higher amounts and $45,000 eventually carried. The issue apparently generated hard feelings and the gap between Dean and the progressive wing subsequently widened. She moved slowly, but inexorably into the pro-developer camp, her comments coming closer to those of Bender and Sawyer. In the wake of Blanchard's untimely demise, that meant a continued 3-3 split on controversial issues whenever Pierce, as he did often if not always, sided with Gorin and Jacobi.

Counting the two-year seat to complete Blanchard's term, five of seven places were up for election in November, and two of the sitting Council Members unexpectedly threw their hats in the ring. Bender had vowed she would not seek a third term, but changed her mind and registered for the special election ballot to fill the remaining part of Blanchard's term. Dean, who had publicly pledged not to run for Council in 2008, withdrew that undertaking and joined Bender on the pro-developer slate.

With progressives sensing an upset in the making and lots of room on the ballot for newcomers, a bruising battle loomed in November 2008 for control of the Santa Rosa City Council.

CHAPTER 3

2008 – END OF AN ERA

"Earthquake" is a good analogy for the transformation of the Santa Rosa political landscape brought about by the City Council elections of 2008. As described above, the ground started shaking in 2006, it moved measurably in 2007, and then *kerbam* – in 2008 for the first time ever, progressives came to power at City Hall with a 4 to 3 majority. How long the new landscape will last remains to be seen, but Santa Rosa's political scenery will not look quite the same again.

The political trend toward progressive support described in the previous chapter accelerated going into the election of 2008. Confrontational rhetoric intensified, labor unions became more involved, campaigns were hard fought, and the tools of Karl Rove-type politicking figured large. Voter concern over both the adequacy of city policies for environmental protection and the influence of developer money surely played the major role in bringing about the eventual progressive victory, but Obama-mania in Santa Rosa made 2008 an unusual year, and fueled an extraordinarily high turnout of registered voters.

Against the background of Obama's historic triumph and the national rejection of Bush/Cheney philosophies, it seems presumptuous to call the Santa Rosa City Council results momentous. But that's what they were for our small corner of the country. This chapter analyzes the 2008 City Council campaign and election results.

2008 – AN EXCEPTIONAL YEAR

2008 was of course an exceptional year at voting booths all across America. In Santa Rosa, 92.4% of registered voters cast ballots, going 3 to 1 for Obama over McCain, passing a ¼ cent sales tax hike to put passenger trains back on local tracks (SMART), and strongly supporting gay and lesbian marriage rights by voting against Proposition 8. The SMART victory was particularly significant for Santa Rosa, which will have two stations on the projected Cloverdale to Larkspur passenger line.

Acrimonious county-level politicking also enlivened the background for Santa Rosa City Council contests in 2008. With two of five County Supervisor seats at stake, pro-developer and progressive forces squared off in bitterly fought campaigns. In District 3, which includes the central slice of Santa Rosa and a high percentage of its residents, non-profit Council on Aging CEO Shirlee Zane took on three-time Santa Rosa Mayor and developer advocate, Sharon Wright, while in west county's District 5, the pro-developer establishment backed young newcomer Efren Carillo against long-time environmentalist Rue Furch.

In Santa Rosa itself, the City Council ballot had a record 15 competitors in two separate races. Eleven candidates were running for four open four-year seats, and four candidates were on a separate ballot entry, vying to complete the two years left on the late Bob Blanchard's term. As in previous years, there were three discernable groups: the growth machine slate; a loosely organized cluster of progressives; and four independents looking to score upsets. As suggested by the "jihad" remark cited at the beginning of this book, the campaigning was more intense than it had been in the recent past, because both sides saw unprecedented potential for change in City Hall policies and programs.

THE GROWTH MACHINE SLATE

On the pro-developer side, candidates had always formed an undeclared slate, but in 2008 for the first time they openly banded together to run as a single unit, calling themselves "The Team." John Sawyer and Jane Bender, both long-time insiders of the establishment electoral machine, led the campaign, joined by fellow City Council incumbent Carol Dean and newcomers Ernesto Olivares and Bobbi Hoff. The latter two had backgrounds favorable to growth coalition interests: Hoff had CPA and business credentials with real estate connections, while Olivares as a career policeman of Latino background gave the slate credibility on law and order issues as well as diversity.

Olivares did not have formal endorsements from his former colleagues in public safety organizations, nor did he have a record of close associations with local Hispanic organizations. Nonetheless, he ran strong on his work with the City's Gang Prevention Task Force and his personal commitment to community involvement in government.

The growth machine election organization mounted a hard-hitting campaign to offset the emotional intensity of its progressive opponents. The slate's political consultant and manager, Herb Williams, put together a slick package including TV spots and full-page newspaper ads with promises to say "no to special interests" and to be "tough" on city budget matters. They stressed the experience

> **"THE TEAM"**
> SLATE FOR CITY COUNCIL ELECTIONS
> 2008
>
> The veterans:
> > John Sawyer – Council incumbent
> > Jane Bender – Council incumbent
>
> The rookies:
> > Carol Dean – appointed Council incumbent
> > Ernesto Olivares – retired SR Police Officer
> > Bobbi Hoff – CPA
>
> The Coach (campaign manager):
> > Herb Williams – political consultant
>
> Major clubhouse backers:
> > Sonoma County Alliance
> > local developers and builders

of the slate's incumbent members, and identified themselves with the Santa Rosa boosterism of their former leader, Bob Blanchard. Endorsements conformed to tradition as North Bay builders and realty groups, supported all five of The Team.

Funding shortfalls in comparison with earlier times appear to have been a major factor in the growth machine's shift to its new approach with an openly declared slate. For one thing, the prime sources of funding had always been developers and the construction industry, both of which were hit especially hard by the recession. Then too, the very costly county supervisor races were also critical to pro-developer interests and doubtless siphoned funds away from the city arena. Consolidation into a slate provided economies from shared advertising and mailers, and perhaps also allowed the "central command" to absorb and/or reduce common costs that might otherwise have been ascribed to individual campaigns.

PROGRESSIVE COALITIONS

In 2008, progressives across the city generally coalesced behind four candidates for the four-year seats: Michael Allen, Marsha Vas Dupre, Gary Wysocky and Lee Pierce. The first three had long been associated with various progressive causes, and Pierce, who won election in 2004 on the pro-developer machine slate, always had a liberal bent and kept open lines to the general public. As noted in the preceding chapter, he had severed his ties with the establishment group, subsequently casting his Council votes more often than not with progressive Council colleagues Gorin and Jacobi.

Marsha Vas Dupre had served on the Council from 1998 to 2002, but was defeated for reelection in 2002, when, as noted above, the establishment and Press Democrat editorial pages joined in strong attacks on her for making an issue of developer campaign financing. She didn't run again in 2004 or 2006, but her continued active participation in a variety of social advocacy organizations and her stint as an elected Santa Rosa Junior College trustee burnished her progressive reputation. This full plate of ongoing community activities stood her in good stead for the 2008 campaign, as did endorsements from the Sierra Club, SCCA, CBSC and Democratic Party organs, among many others.

Wysocky and Allen also both had solid progressive records. An avid cyclist, Wysocky had taken up civic activism only a few years earlier, but then quickly made his mark as a founder of the Sonoma County Bicycle Coalition and advocate for green transportation. Throughout the campaign, Wysocky's support team emphasized "knocking on doors," and the resulting personalized outreach accounted in large part for his first-place finish. The public contact also convinced him that many citizens felt alienated from local officialdom, so he made neighborhood issues a priority, and pledged to work for more inclusive and responsive government.

As for Allen, of all the candidates he was perhaps the best qualified on paper for a Council job by virtue of his long involvement in civic affairs as a lawyer and mediator, albeit primarily as a labor union official. He had strong support not only from labor and Democrats, but also endorsements from environmentalist organizations, including the Sierra Club. His low-key style, earnest personality and logical positions, however, failed to make a strong enough impression on the electorate, and he finished well behind the leaders.

Finally, most progressives welcomed Pierce into their fold. He was endorsed by key progressive political organizations, namely CCSR, CBSC and Democratic Party units, but he did not have a close enough past association with environmentalists to draw on that wing for significant campaign support. Hewing to his independent image, Pierce also declined to make explicit platform pledges requested by some organizations and consequently did not garner public endorsements from unions, although a number worked quietly to help his campaign along.

Two progressives entered the race for the two-year seat: Judy Kennedy and David Rosas. Both had fine records of civic activism and solid backing from progressive groupings, although the danger was evident to all that the two would take votes from each other and thereby ease the path for their pro-developer opponent, Jane Bender. Lacking

GARY WYSOCKY
PROGRESSIVE COUNCIL
MEMBER, VICE MAYOR-2010

A CPA with his own business, Gary Wysocky served as President of the Junior College Neighborhood Association, was a founding Board Member and President of the Sonoma County Bicycle Coalition, and an active member of Friends of SMART. He has also taught at Sonoma State University and Piner High School.

Voters resonated to his forceful personality and messages of neighborhood involvement, environmental stewardship, and fiscal responsibility. On his first-time run for City elected office, Wysocky beat out incumbent Mayor John Sawyer to finish at the head of the pack.

On the Council, Wysocky has been a strong advocate for alternative transportation and community engagement. He has also taken the lead with CPA-style probing into fiscal issues, in particular on the budget, but also as a lead voice on big ticket items like terms for the trash-hauling franchise and justification for financing of the downtown garage project.

a central organization to "select" their standard bearers, progressives found no consensus solution to the dilemma of having two candidates for the same seat. It would have been difficult in any case to defeat Bender, a two-term incumbent and former Mayor with strong name recognition – in the end she outpolled the combined total of both progressives, although marked on fewer than 50% of all ballots.

All six progressive candidates campaigned on similar platforms and often shared the same spotlight, but they did not have unitary organizational backing nor did they run as a slate. They all had been active in grassroots organizations, and all been boosters of environmental protection, social justice, and local commerce. Organizations like the Sierra Club, Sonoma County Conservation Action, Concerned Citizens for Santa Rosa, and the Coalition for a Better Sonoma County gave their traditional support to progressive candidates.

Organized labor and the local Democratic Party took more active roles than in past years. Labor lined up strongly behind Allen with funding and canvassing help. Unions also gave moral support to other progressive candidates for the Council, although they did not steer much financial help directly to individual campaigns except for Allen. Union contributions for independent expenditure mailers were, however, substantial for the Council races, even if in the larger picture most union money and sweat went into county supervisor campaigns where health care and employee benefit issues loomed large.

The Sonoma County Democratic Party Central Committee also made its preferences for progressives known. So did several other local Democratic Party organs, impelled in part by national Party efforts to reach down into the grassroots as part of new-style campaigning for Obama. Senator Pat Wiggins and Assembly Member Noreen Evans gave personal endorsements and Evans chipped in with money from her campaign war chest.

2008 – THE ISSUES

Campaign efforts to frame the election agenda for voters followed predictable patterns. Progressives, with differing individual emphasis, highlighted their commitment to environmental protection, community issues and neighborhood involvement. In this vein, they identified themselves with environmental and economic "sustainability," a term that while often ambiguous, usually focused attention on new approaches to transportation and energy challenges. Progressives also stressed commitments to the goals of numerous local non-profits dedicated to environmental and social justice issues, while criticizing "The Team" for its connections to developers and pointing to the responsibility of recent Councils for policies that aggravated budget problems.

The growth machine slate, under its The Team banner, stressed the experience of its leading members, along with support for a healthy economy and for public safety. These priorities echoed candidates' personal associations with past Council actions and with organizations such as the Sonoma County Alliance and Santa Rosa Chamber of Commerce. Members of The Team also promised to make "the tough decisions" necessary in the budget crisis, proposing 10% cuts in city employee salaries across the board, although they tended to ignore the fact that the only short-term way around legally binding contracts was negotiations with city employees for voluntary concessions, an ongoing process at the time. Overall, the slate tried hard to distance itself from "special interests" and to get on the environmental bandwagon – themes that opponents charged were inconsistent with the record, if not downright disingenuous.

The unaffiliated candidates typically presented themselves as strong and savvy individual leaders, beholden to no group. Only one of them, Don Taylor, proved competitive. Taylor, a local restaurant owner and leader in rehabilitating the city's Railroad Square district, had a foot in both main camps, but ran on his own record, expressing personal priority for the local economy and public safety. He did well, coming in sixth in the eleven-candidate race for the regular four-year term.

Not surprisingly, much of the rhetoric from all parties was pitched in general terms to promise results "when elected." Unlike 2006, there were no killer "hit pieces," although several campaign mailers on both sides were sharply worded. Clashes between candidates at public campaign forums tended to focus on past City Council decisions or positions taken by incumbent candidates during their time of service. At such events, however, few points appeared to have been scored on policy issues, although individual candidates doubtless gained or lost votes based on the personal impressions they were able to convey to audiences.

The Press Democrat harped on the budget and labor unions. The paper took progressive candidates to task for signing pledges to support laws on labor unions, and asserted "growth" was no longer an issue. These themes reinforced the growth machine campaign approach with its emphasis on readiness to take "tough decisions," and equating labor to "special interests," somehow on par with developers. The term "special interests" is in fact widely used to refer to any group that seeks to influence public officeholders, but it raises the loudest alarm bells with reference to those, such as developers or contractors, who stand to make personal financial gains from Council actions favoring their projects. On the other side, advocates for environmental protection, better wages, affordable housing and diversity generally do not stand to profit personally from Council decisions supportive of the causes they espouse.

The Press Democrat's treatment

2008 – ELECTION RESULTS	
Total ballots cast: 72,453	
For four-year terms (voters marked up to four names, totaling about 212,000 boxes marked all together)	
Gary Wysocky	29,018
John Sawyer	27,870
Ernesto Olivares	26,288
Marsha Vas Dupre	23,894
Lee Pierce	22,037
Don Taylor	21,262
Michael Allen	18,974
Bobbi Hoff	15,622
Carol Dean	14,013
Eddie Alvarez	7,601
Hans Dippel	4,905
For a two year term about 57,900 ballots marked (voters marked only one name)	
Jane Bender	26,425
Judy Kennedy	12,342
David Rosas	11,372
Lawrence R Wiesner	7,866
Source: Sonoma County Registrar of Voters website	

of the labor issue was decidedly partisan in favor of The Team. While the paper criticized Allen, Wysocky and Dupre for taking the labor pledge, it failed on every occasion to also draw attention to the political role of major City employee union leaders, who were active on the Sonoma County Alliance Political Action Committee that worked on behalf of all five of The Team candidates. Separately, representatives of the five major city employee unions endorsed Sawyer, Bender, Dean, Pierce and Allen.

Without access to results of targeted exit polling, it is difficult to say how many votes can be ascribed to a Press Democrat endorsement. In 2008, the paper backed three of The Team – Sawyer, Olivares and Bender – and two progressives Wysocky and Pierce. Come election day, that gave it a fine record of four "wins" of five seats. On the other hand, the paper's continuous carping attacks on Dupre did not prevent her election, and the editorial board endorsements were generally given to those candidates who were already leading in the pre-election polls.

WHAT MADE THE DIFFERENCE?

What do the results tell us about "the people's will?" Judging from the messages put out during the campaign by the successful candidates, the strongest undercurrent was public desire that city policies be based more on environmental sustainability, and less on special interests. Those were themes winning progressives Wysocky and Dupre put up front in their campaigns. The three victorious candidates from The Team, as noted above, also ran on a platform advocating environmental protection and promising to say "no to special interests."

If one looks at geographic distribution, a split between the wealthier suburbs and the rest of the city was also evident, although margins were only rarely very great in any of the city's voting districts. Sawyer, Bender and Olivares all ran well in the northeast – Fountaingrove, Montecito Heights, etc. – and Oakmont. These areas lean conservative (which in Sonoma County is of course not very conservative compared to the rest of the country), tend to favor candidates with clear establishment ties like those of Sawyer and Bender, and would presumably have been attracted to Olivares for his police and gang-taskforce credentials.

Wysocky and Dupre along with progressive colleagues scored well in most central and southern precincts. This area covers a variety of economic backgrounds from the firmly middle class older areas around Santa Rosa Junior College to the mix of newer subdivisions and lower income sections south of Highway 12. The neighborhoods there have been sources of civic activism stemming from discontent over environmental and social justice or diversity issues.

Money appears to have been an important factor, with progressives outpacing pro-developer candidates in individual campaign contributions. Developer and construction industry donations to individuals were down considerably from previous years, presumably due largely to the recession – part of the difference was clearly made up by the economies of running a unified slate and some of the campaign costs may have been absorbed by the Williams organization, which has given discounts to candidates and does not apparently charge for such items as polling. According to campaign finance reports, the top three progressives (Michael Allen at $68,849, Marsha Vas Dupre at $64,848, and Gary Wysocky at $55,477) spent about twice as much as their principal rivals (Ernesto Olivares at $34,975, Jane Bender at $31,816 and John Sawyer at $22,344).[9] Labor union money went principally to Allen and to help fund IE (independent expenditures) mailers supporting the four progressives in the four-year race.

The engagement of labor unions and the Democratic Party also helped progressives significantly, especially with name recognition. The several Democratic clubs and party committees spread good words about progressives within their networks, and the unions contributed funds to enable more far-reaching IE mailers than in past years. The increased inputs from these quarters went far to offset the advantages pro-developer candidates have enjoyed from Press Democrat support, more professional campaign materials and mailers, and extensive sign placements.

The high turn-out may also have been a factor, since Democrats are typically progressive, and they came out in full force to vote for Obama. One cannot make too much of this, however, since many voters did not go on down the ballot to mark choices for City Council races. In Santa Rosa, over 72,000 registered voters cast ballots and presumably nearly all put down their choices for President, but of the total only about 58,000 marked their ballots for the two-year Council term.

No matter how one analyzes the fine points, it is hard to escape the conclusion that the post-2006 realignments on the Santa Rosa City Council followed from disenchantment with the elitist style and pro-developer policies adopted for years by growth machine Council majorities. Lee Pierce spearheaded the change by his actions in Council chambers, and voters completed the mini-revolution by their action inside election booths. Citizens, it seemed, had become more concerned about greenhouse gases and social programs than promotion of high-rises, fancy suburbs and big-box stores. The implications of climate change, the economic crunch and city budget woes, immigration and the backlash against it – these and related issues all became part of the mix, even though there is as yet no strong consensus on measures to be taken for resolution of these problems.

THE COUNTY PARALLEL

In 2008, the especially hard fight between pro-developer forces and progressives overlapped in both city and county, playing out in very intense political struggles for the two open Sonoma County Supervisor seats. In the 5th (west county) District, a long-time environmentalist leader, Rue Furch, was upset by Efren Carrillo, a relatively young and inexperienced Santa Rosan, who effectively used the financial backing of the pro-developer establishment and also proved himself a strong door-knocking campaigner. Most observers ascribed Furch's loss to revelations that she had been late in making tax payments, an issue Carrillo was able to exploit with the de facto partisan support of the Press Democrat, which repeatedly hammered Furch on the point.

It was the 3rd District (central Santa Rosa and Rohnert Park) supervisor race, however, that cast the longest shadow over the City Council contests. It had a touch of David and Goliath – Sharon Wright, as former Santa Rosa Mayor and principal cog in the city's growth machine for two decades, embodied all the success and power of the establishment. She had finished first in every Council race she entered and served a record three stints as Mayor. For her part, Shirlee Zane had never held an elected office here, although as CEO of the Council on Aging, she had accrued strong progressive credentials and good name recognition.

Wright's defeat was significant. She had sought – unsuccessfully – to recast herself as an environmentalist and non-profit advocate, while attacking Zane for ties to labor unions. Zane counterpunched by highlighting Wright's developer connections, her record of paring back environmental protections, and her flip-flops of political party registration from Democrat to Republican and back. On the positive side, Zane stressed the need for new approaches, and ran on her own demonstrably progressive record, emphasizing issues such as environmental protection, health care, senior advocacy and improved transportation. She scored a decisive win.

THE POLITICS OF IT ALL

The political shifts of 2008 carried a message that voters want more attention to environmental protection and quality of life issues. In the first instance, the change of attitudes seems to have come about simply because large numbers of Santa Rosans are thinking people, who have reevaluated what they see around them and what they think the city's government should be doing. In the deeper background, generational change may also be part of the picture, and perhaps more importantly, the major influx of new people over the past two or three decades seems to have resulted in a higher percentage of those concerned with social and environmental issues.

In 2007, then-Mayor Bob Blanchard, speaking from his perspective as leader of the pro-developer Council majority, in effect complained about the attitudes of relative newcomers He pointed out that Santa Rosa had become the fifth largest city in the North Bay, and "observed that the people who are now the most vociferous opponents of growth, the most vocal about the problems, are those who have lived here less than seven years."[10] Indeed, intensified urbanization of both the city and county has brought more cosmopolitan mindsets and less willingness to "go with the flow" of continuous auto-centric growth. Gaye LeBaron captured a sense of the difference from the old days when she noted in her column on Blanchard's remarks, "If anyone had suggested that there would be lawsuits over a parking garage at the Junior College, he would have been laughed at."

In any case, Santa Rosans are concerned to do their part for greenhouse gas reductions, energy efficiency, and more sustainable development in general. In the same vein, they worry that even when the economy recovers resumption of old style suburban growth with its overtones of sprawl and more intensive infill development will stress natural resources like water, worsen traffic woes and fail to address demographic change.

The question of what to do next, however, does not have a simple answer. Clearly, much work has to be done to put the local economy and city revenues on a stronger footing. Innovation, promoting local enterprises, going green and launching SMART hold great promise and appear to many as critical ingredients for a sustainable future. But a substantial number of citizens are wary of radical change and still look to big box stores, a revival of the construction industry and auto-dependent development as key for some time to come.

What does this mix of concerns mean for local politics, and what strategies will local politicians use to seek popular support and the power to govern that goes with it? The next four chapters step back for a more in-depth analysis of what drives politics in our fair city. Chapters 4 and 5 look at the interests that inspire the growth machine and its broader pro-developer alliances, while Chapters 6 and 7 examine the dynamics of progressive coalitions.

RECAP – THE ROAD TO A PROGRESSIVE MAJORITY

SANTA ROSA CITY COUNCIL ELECTION & APPOINTMENT RESULTS 2002-2008			
YEAR	WINNERS	FACTION	POST-ELECTION LINE-UP
2002			
	Rabinowitsh	Progressive:	
	Blanchard	Pro-developer	
	Condron	Pro-developer	
			Pro-dev. 5 vs. Progressive 2
2004			
	Bender	Pro-developer	
	Martini	Pro-developer	
	Sawyer	Pro-developer	
	Pierce	Pro-developer	
			Pro-dev. 6 vs. Progressive 1
2006			
	Gorin	Progressive	
	Blanchard	Pro-developer	
	Jacobi	Progressive	
			Pro-dev. 5 vs. Progressive 2

2007 -no election			
	Dean-appointed	Non-affiliated	
	Pierce-incumbent.	Leaves pro-developer	
			Pro-dev. 3, Progressive 2, Non-affiliated 2,
2008 pre-election			
	Blanchard	Resigned-not replaced	
	Dean	Moves to pro-developer	
	Pierce	Moves to progressive	
			Pro-dev. 3 vs. Progressive 3
2008			
	Wysocky	Progressive	
	Dupre	Progressive	
	Sawyer	Pro-developer	
	Bender	Pro-developer	
	Olivares	Pro-developer	
			Progressive 4 vs. Pro-dev. 3

Chapter 4

The Politics of Place and Money that Talks[11]

Is there an underlying pattern that will help to better understand and describe Santa Rosa's political dynamics? Social scientists across America have given much thought to how governments function in our cities, big and small – the "politics of place," as the topic has been called. Although US cities are exceptionally diverse in age, size, location, climate, economy, and population, there are many common forces at work among the groups of people active in the contest to control decision-making authority at City Hall.

In America, elected City Councils control how land parcels will be used or developed. Millions of dollars in profits or losses ride on their decisions and that being the case, there is typically one smallish group – developers and associated land interests – that has the motivation and money to mount campaigns year after year to elect sympathetic city council members. These individuals who stand to benefit financially from land development decisions catalyze "growth machines," which become the proverbial 800-pound gorilla, using their wealth to out-muscle the combined forces of other interest groups that weave in and out of city politics, but lack comparable resources and staying power to compete effectively.

The abiding American faith in continuous growth has helped development-oriented growth machines to create "urban regimes" – alliances between elected governments and developer interest groups to shape the making of city policy. Powerful and lasting coalitions emerge to promote intensified land development in particular, and population expansion in general. Environmentalists, neighborhood defenders and others have periodically opposed specific development projects and more generally have resisted sprawl for some years now. Only recently, however, has public opinion began to give serious consideration to evidence that the growth ethic has its limits, and the time has come to adopt new approaches to land-use and resource exploitation.

This chapter reviews central themes of urban political dynamics to set the broad framework for analysis of Santa Rosa politics. Although the discussion that follows draws heavily on academic sources, it is a layman's common sense application without pretension to scholarly rigor. The chapter after this one will move from the general to the specific – to describe the political machine supported by Santa Rosa land-development interests that through 2006 elected controlling majorities to our City Council.

LAND AND POLITICAL POWER STRUCTURES

Land is a special commodity. Its supply is strictly limited, it is not movable, and enormous profits hinge on local government permissions for how it can or cannot be developed. Academics refer to the worth of land in two broad categories: its "exchange value," which comes from trading it for monetary payments, and its "use value," which comes from assigning it uses to meet social needs not keyed to monetary income. The latter concept – use value – encompasses the importance that people ascribe to how land is used for daily needs and quality of life, including the creation of public parks and open spaces, the protection of

> ### TYPICAL GROWTH COALITION MEMBERSHIP
> ******
>
> Land or place entrepreneurs
> -land owner-developers
> -inherited land owners
> -property renters
>
> Land financiers
> -banks
> -mortgage companies
>
> Population growth interests
> -real estate brokers
> -gas and electric companies
> -telephone and cable companies
> -large businesses
>
> "Growth is good" boosters
> -local newspaper
> -chamber of commerce

neighborhoods to retain familiar and comfortable surroundings, the preservation of historic districts, and provision of sites for churches or affordable housing. In the same vein, use value also derives from the denial of land to polluting or people-unfriendly facilities.[12]

In contrast to those kinds of social land uses, the term "exchange value" speaks to the generation of wealth through purchase, development and sale of land. By extension, the concept takes in related economic activities, such as payments collected by landlords, realtors, mortgage lenders, real estate lawyers, title companies and so forth. In an urban setting, profits typically derive from development of the land through construction of residential or commercial facilities, or through other improvements to the surrounding areas that increase buyer interest in the land.

The profit potential of land is an ever-present basis for formation of local power elites. The celebrated author of *Who Rules America*, University of California at Santa Cruz Professor G. William Domhoff has observed, "Power structures at the city level are different from the national power structure…A local power structure is at its core an aggregate of land-based interests that profit from increasingly intensive use of land."[13] Coalitions form based on the obvious economic interest – those who own land or have the wealth to buy it, seek development of that land in order to produce more wealth from the sale or future use of that land.

Profits from land hinge on decisions made by local governments, and that fact generates a powerful incentive for wealthy elites to back growth-supporters for election to municipal and county-level governing bodies. In American cities, as in Santa Rosa, City Councils or equivalent elected bodies set the city's general development direction and make the ultimate decisions on land-use. Council members also pick planning commissioners and name individuals to seats on utility, parking, transit, water and design review boards, which in turn implement policies to facilitate development and give the approvals needed for specific projects.[14]

The vigorous mobilization of growth-promotion elites generally gives them influence on city policy greatly disproportionate to their numbers. Their success in electing allies to city councils and gaining appointments of their associates to the key municipal boards and commissions mentioned above squeezes out representation from other sectors of the social fabric. Many professions, teachers, middle class workers in general, minorities, low-income residents, and so on have as a rule had little or no voice in their local government compared to that enjoyed by development and business elites.[15]

URBAN REGIMES

A successful growth coalition can maintain government control for years. Sustained cooperation between city officials and particular interest groups constitutes an "urban regime," defined in the now-canonical writings of Clarence Stone from the University of Maryland as "the informal arrangements by which public bodies and private interests function together and carry out governing decisions." [16] One major variation on the theme described by Stone is the "developmental regime," which has the principal objectives of promoting growth and preventing economic decline. Such a "marriage" between local government and business is common because city officials perceive needs for economic growth that generate revenue, and alliances between developers and business elites can provide complementing resources and expertise to advance those goals.

The closest collaborators with developers are financiers and construction industry executives. Many larger development firms both buy land and undertake construction on it. Building material supply companies are also natural allies, as are those builders who may not regularly purchase the land, but rely heavily on contracts with developers.

The land-owning nucleus with its financial backers is also joined in political endeavors by a range of ready partners who stand to profit from the secondary effects of growth. These represent interests that benefit not so much from the intensification of land use *per se*, but from the associated increase in population that comes with land development. Gas, electric, telephone and cable TV companies, for example, want to broaden their customer base. So too, do local branches of national retail chains and larger local businesses with ambitions to expand. Smaller businesses and those with neighborhood focus may be more ambivalent, although they often participate in hopes of benefiting from a "good business climate." Museums, theaters, and universities may also support growth on grounds that attracting more people to move into the area will help fill their halls and classrooms.

Chambers of Commerce are typically a powerful force on the front lines of growth promotion. Chambers as a rule equate population growth to business opportunity and hence are usually quick to support most, if not necessarily all, development projects. A local Chamber is, moreover, often a key venue for networking among the business elite, a training ground for business-oriented local political leaders, and at election time, an amplifier of support for pro-growth policies with or without endorsing specific candidates.

Then too, "there is one other important component of the local growth coalition: the daily newspaper," noted Domhoff in his 2005 essay. He cites a former publisher of the San Jose Mercury News, who, when asked why he had so strongly favored development that was clear-cutting the old orchards around the city, famously replied, "Trees do not read newspapers." It may not be as simple as that in every case, and daily newspapers may diverge from pro-growth colleagues to oppose one or another specific development project or electoral candidate. Their need to appeal to a broader constituency requires them to play a more "statesman-like" and flexible role, but at the end of the day, they have generally consistent track records of actively participating in pro-developer coalitions to advance the cause of growth and growth-minded electoral candidates. Santa Rosa's Press Democrat is no exception.

Labor unions may or may not partner closely with growth machines. Particular unions may sign on to growth promotion in expectation that development will create jobs for their members. On the other hand, a significant proportion of jobs, for example in any given construction project, may be temporary in nature or primarily low wage. Also, pro-developer leaders generally oppose negotiation of specific labor-related benefit standards for development or construction contracts. That has become a hot issue in Sonoma County, where the construction industry has vociferously fought Community Benefits Agreements or similar arrangements that might require union shops or set wage floors. In sum, while labor has an obvious interest in jobs associated with development, the choice to give political support to pro-developer politicians may require downplaying traditional labor concerns like affordable housing, health care and living wage ordinances.

Finally, it should be noted that growth coalitions are not always unified in pursuit of short term objectives. Members may disagree over timing or location of any given project or phase of city development, competing head-on to obtain a project approval or deny one for a competitor. Then too, developers may have to choose between governmental jurisdictions that have lined up one against the other to attract projects or big box stores with potential for tax-producing revenue. Generally, however, the underlying belief in sustained urban growth holds development coalitions together at the city and county levels.

IN GROWTH WE TRUST(ED)

Until recently, most Americans have warmly accepted the idea that economic growth is sustainable forever and good for everybody. Edwin Stennett titled his popular 2002 book "In Growth We Trust"[17] to capture the common notion that growth is synonymous with beneficial progress — the book itself is a ringing indictment of sprawl and pro-developer political machines in the Chesapeake Bay region. The elite who benefit the most from increased land exploitation work to exploit the popular faith in never-ending growth, and are often able to co-opt civic pride, turning it into growth-serving boosterism that promotes urban expansion and champions efforts to attract new businesses of all types.

Is economic growth in the 21st century necessary for, or

> ### SHARON WRIGHT
> ### FORMER MAYOR - GROWTH MACHINE LEADER
>
> As a City Council Member from 1992 to 2004, Sharon Wright held the post of Mayor for an unmatched three times. She also served extensively on Bay area transportation-related boards, and among other community activities, volunteered in support of Memorial Hospital
>
> At the same time, she retained close working relationships with developers, the Sonoma County Alliance and the SR Chamber of Commerce — so close in fact that the California Fair Political Practices Commission fined her $14,500 in 1998 for conflict of interest and failing to disclose income from those two organizations. Wright's career appears a textbook example of the side-by-side connection that can emerge between government officials and developer interests. That image would seem to have been a major reason for her 2008 failure to win election as a County Supervisor.
>
> As of 2010, Wright continues to serve on the Sonoma County Alliance Political Action Committee and has her own PR consulting firm in Santa Rosa.

even likely to bring, prosperity? No – at least not in the traditional way – but the perception persists that growth can still somehow automatically bring more people, more jobs, more security, and more opportunities for all concerned. Believers hold that unevenness will be ironed out over time, and if some people fail to obtain their fair share on the prosperity scale, tangible benefits will nonetheless accrue to the majority. And indeed, much of the American experience, notably in the generally prosperous half century following World War II, has seemed to confirm this broad thesis.

But that is not the whole story. In its initial phases, growth at the local level will usually generate jobs in the construction industry and in the case of new business centers, follow-on employment. Studies have shown, however, that although employment may spurt with a rush of development, unemployment within the immediate area goes down very little if at all and "in the long run, if you create five jobs, four of them go to people who would otherwise be living somewhere else."[18] One has to ask also whether the new jobs pay well or poorly, and how any new influx of people and business activity, such as shopping malls, will impact traffic congestion, infrastructure costs, demands for expensive public safety and medical services, affordable housing needs and degradation of the local environment. Later chapters will return to these and other concerns, which have led local jurisdictions to impose impact fees and growth controls.

Many also believe that growth is necessary to generate taxes and fees to keep up with increasing demands on city budgets. In many places, especially California owing to its infamous Proposition 13, there is such a high premium on any addition of new sales tax revenue that city governments may downplay problems, provide subsidies to development projects and engage in throat-cutting competition with neighboring towns for big box and other retail establishments. A true assessment, however, must be based on whether the revenue from a new business, for example from a big box store, does in fact cover the costs of additional city services and is not offset by taking away from local businesses in a saturated market. Total sales tax proceeds may not go up at all if a new retailer merely puts existing retailers out of business.

Population growth is often used as short-hand for economic growth, but it is flat wrong to conclude that economic growth requires a population increase. As far back as 1972, the prestigious national Rockefeller Commission on "Population Growth and the American Future" concluded: "The health of our country does not depend on population growth, nor does the vitality of business, nor the welfare of the average person." The report did little, however, to slow population growth in the US, which grew from 210 million people in 1972 to 296 million in 2005 (41%). For comparison, Japan grew 19% and Germany only 4% over the same years and their economies reached comparatively prosperous levels. A Brookings Institution paper published in 2002 covering the 100 largest US metropolitan areas through the 1990s confirmed the point with convincing data that in the words of the author, "punctured one important piece of conventional wisdom: the idea that achieving income growth in a metropolitan area requires population growth." [19]

SANTA ROSA AND THE AMERICAN DREAM

Santa Rosa plunged whole-heartedly into the post-World War II pursuit of growth. Prosperity followed thanks to the acumen and enterprise of its business community leaders, who in the years following 1945 put together an ambitious plan for expansion and garnered public support for their vision of a "city designed for living."[20] Streets were extended and utilities improved; merchants made sure Highway 101 stayed smack in the center of town to deliver customers right to their stores; and new land parcels were opened to accommodate suburbs with a car (or two) in every garage.

Santa Rosa town fathers – and they were males for a long time – were a resourceful bunch. They fundraised for a hospital, introduced a special district in the 1950s to fund downtown parking facilities, attracted a Sears store, established a Redevelopment Agency in 1961 when downtown began to go to seed; and came up with resources to build anew after the destructive earthquake of 1969. On the way they annexed Montgomery Village, nearly doubling the Santa Rosa's population in one stroke; absorbed numerous other swaths of land into the town's orbit; brought in the Santa Rosa Plaza Mall; and in many less spectacular ways shepherded the maturation of a regional government, retail, and service center.

The Santa Rosa version of the ubiquitous American growth coalition emerged in the 1950s. As Gaye LeBaron and Joann Mitchell wrote, "The political power of the country was shifting away from the agricultural forces and the merchants, spelling the end of Santa Rosa as a farm town. The new politics belonged to the men who were financing the building boom."[21] These barons of finance, development and construction not only fueled the building boom, they also underwrote the city's cultural life, promoted its schools, and delineated its moral standards while smoothly assuming the reins of political power to set city policies.

Such disagreement as did arise came mostly from within the elite. Men with strong egos and drive naturally produced plenty of competition and differing views. The most famous clash arose when Santa Rosa's legendary native son developer, Hugh Codding, fought the city to stop the Santa Rosa Plaza Mall in hopes of preserving a dominant position for his Coddingtown Mall not far to the north. He lost and had to pay millions for the settlement, though he soon recovered, prospered and remained a major influence in the city. Through all such turbulence, the unifying forces of the belief in continuous growth kept Santa Rosa on its course of expansion and development.

THE SONOMA COUNTY ALLIANCE VS. "ENVIROS"

In the 1960s, however, a backlash against free-wheeling urban development had germinated in Sonoma County. Rachel Carson's seminal book, *Silent Spring,* appeared in 1962, about the time that grassroots activism swelled here in Sonoma County to assure cancellation of plans to build a nuclear power station in Bodega Bay and later to successfully promote public access to the California coast. In Santa Rosa itself, there were initial mild demonstrations of concern in the 1970s when Hewlett Packard initiated its proposal to build a facility in the essentially undeveloped Fountaingrove Ranch area on the city's northeastern edge. Opposition to HP soon faded, however, and local environmentalists focused more on habitat and open land preservation with public access than on developments inside Santa Rosa's city limits.

Still, the increasing pressure for stronger environmental protection measures worried developers and spurred the founding in 1974 of the Sonoma County Alliance (SCA). The Alliance was formed primarily as a lobbying organization for the development community, including among its objectives defense of private property rights and influence on the political process. It also had substantial participation from agricultural interests and over time broadened its agenda to attract not only a range of business people, but also labor union representatives and some government officials.

Environmental and other progressive activism, however, continued to grow. Political competition between the developer community and progressives heated up in the 1980s as the latter moved to counter the growing influence of SCA on the local scene. Dick Day united with several leading progressives in 1986 to found Concerned Citizens for Santa Rosa (CCSR). Joining forces, Day and Petaluma environmental activist, Bill Kortum, in 1991 worked to establish Sonoma County Conservation Action (SCCA), which in short order became a leading political force to promote environmentalist candidates and progressive issues.

For its part, SCA intensified efforts to support its favored candidates for local government and to promote ballot measures of interest to its primary development and business constituencies. In 1990, it contributed $5,500 to candidates for city councils and county supervisors, and another $5,000 to advance a sales tax initiative that would have supported widening of Highway 101.[22] The highway measure came close to passing, but concerted opposition led by environmentalists ensured its defeat.

By 1990, the battle lines were clearly drawn between the two camps. On the one side stood developers and their pro-growth allies; and on the other, environmentalists and their progressive soul mates. For its 1990 road tax effort to fund expansion of Highway 101, the pro-developer coalition hired a Sacramento-based pollster named Herb Williams. Williams decided he liked the territory, moved to Santa Rosa in 1992, and promptly helped turn the pro-developer coalition into a smoothly-oiled political machine. The next chapter looks into how it works.

CHAPTER 5

MACHINE POLITICS – SANTA ROSA STYLE

The commanding presence of Santa Rosa's long-dominant growth machine was outlined by Press Democrat columnist Chris Coursey in late 2006 when he wrote: "...consider the political reality. Bender and Bob Blanchard and Mike Martini and John Sawyer and the folks who have made up the majority of the Council for at least the past decade control the power in city politics. The city moves in the direction they want it to, which usually coincides with the business and development interests that dominate their base of support and supply the campaign money that keeps them in office."[23] That changed for the first time in 2007/8 as described above in Chapters 2 and 3.

The task of this chapter is to describe this political machine, which remains a formidable force working to regain its 'top-dog' position. How is it organized to provide essential continuity? Where do the funds come from year after year? Who selects the candidates, assembles the resources, steers the money to the right places and leads the troops into campaign battles? And does the loss of absolute City Council control in 2008 suggest the machine is running out of gas or just retooling?

The appraisal here of Santa Rosa's growth machine will be followed in the next two chapters by examination of the other side in city politics – the loosely connected factions noted in preceding sections as "progressives."

SANTA ROSA'S POLITICAL MACHINE

Though it failed to gain a Council majority in 2008, Santa Rosa's pro-developer political machine has all the major features necessary for continued professional team performance. There is organizational continuity, an experienced "coach," alliances with community business elites, a message appealing to many voters, and the all-important ingredient …money. Although the local pro-developer machine is embedded in a county-wide network, this chapter will address primarily the elements that operate to support candidates for the Santa Rosa City Council, namely campaign manager Herb Williams at the core, the Sonoma County Alliance, the broader coalition of growth advocates, and the machine's major funding sources.

The Sonoma County Alliance (SCA) is the organizational 'home' for the political activities of the pro-developer community. It has been called the "most influential business lobby in the North Bay" [24] – it has boasted both close connections to City Hall and a membership with many of the county's wealthiest firms. As of early 2009, SCA counted 350 members, described on its website[25] as a "coalition of business, agriculture, labor and individuals incorporated to encourage a healthy economy, maintain a sound environment, protect private property rights and promote a responsive political process." SCA has a full-time Executive Director and main committees for Political Action, Infrastructure, the Environment and Transportation.

"The Alliance," in its own words, "accomplishes (its) goals through public and member education and, from time to time, through advocacy before decision makers." The Political Action Committee (PAC or SCAPAC) and Executive Committee members maintain contacts with city leaders, and there is a general membership meeting monthly (at 7:30 am) for informational programs. SCA's major public service project is "Take Back Our Community," which seeks to help reduce violent crime through a "monetary reward fund to assist local law enforcement and the District Attorney's Office to bring such (criminals) to justice."

Judging from its membership, SCA's bedrock interests accentuate the development, construction and finance sectors. Its member directory includes virtually all the leading local organizations of those industries: Northbay Realtors Association, North Coast Builders Exchange,

Northern Division of the Homebuilders Association, North Coast Rental Housing Association, Engineering Contractors Association, the Santa Rosa Chamber of Commerce, and PG & E. Operating Engineers Local No. 3 (the largest construction trades local in the United States) is also on the list along with the Sonoma County Farm Bureau, "the voice of agricultural producers," which has been an influential actor in SCA since its beginnings.

The "Big 3" of Santa Rosa's municipal employees unions are also politically active players within SCA. The Santa Rosa Fire Fighters Association, the Santa Rosa Police Officers Association, and the city's largest union, the SR City

---

SONOMA COUNTY ALLIANCE PRO-DEVELOPER POLITICAL ACTION BASE -- 2010*

Executive Director – Lisa Shaffner
Healdsburg City Council Member 1999-2008
-twice serving as Mayor
+++
Political Action Committee (PAC) with 25 trustees, including representation from:

Real estate development:
    Christopherson Homes (2 members)
    Airport Business Center
    Quaker Hill Development
    Korman Development
    Tuxhorn Company
    Stewart Title Company
Finance
    Wells Fargo Bank
    Sequoia Pacific Mortgage
Builders
    Home Builders Association
    North Coast Builders Exchange
SR City employee associations
    Santa Rosa City Employees Association
    Santa Rosa Police Officers (2)
    Santa Rosa Fire Fighters

* information from sonomacountyalliance. com/ accessed February 15, 2010

Employees Association (SRCEA), are members of SCA and all three unions have representatives on the SCA Political Action Committee. The Chairman of that committee through the campaign and elections of 2008 was Tony Alvernaz, President of SRCEA. The Sonoma County Sheriffs Association is also in the membership directory. These leaders of employee unions and officer associations have seen it in their best interests to collaborate with the powers that be, namely SCA and its allies, who have for many years backed the winning side in City Council elections – Council members are, of course, the officials who ultimately approve city employee wages and benefits.

SCA's political effectiveness has been manifest in its choice of Executive Directors. The current (Feb. 2010) incumbent is Lisa Schaffner, a Healdsburg City Council Member from 1999 to 2008, including two terms as Mayor, and membership at varying times on important Sonoma County governmental committees. Two former SCA Executive Directors served simultaneously as Mayor of Santa Rosa: Mike Martini who preceded Schaffner and Sharon Wright, who is still a Trustee on the SCA Political Action Committee. Wright, as noted in the previous chapter (textbox) was fined $14,500 by the California Fair Political Practices Commission in 1998 for 10 violations, including failure to report income from SCA while serving on the Santa Rosa City Council.[26]

The hard core inside SCA is its sharply focused political apparatus, dedicated to "organizing for more effective political actions." The primary coordinating mechanism to get the job done is its Political Action Committee, which works to shape the local political agenda and lobby for SCA goals. When political campaign seasons open, SCAPAC interviews, endorses and provides campaign contributions to selected candidates for offices in Sonoma County. SCA's Executive Director helps recruit candidates to run on election slates and canvass members for campaign contributions.

THE "KARL ROVE OF SANTA ROSA"

The SCA-led coalition morphed into a finely-tuned political machine in the early 1990s when Herb Williams joined the group as its election campaign coordinator and political consultant. In the eyes of his political opponents, Williams is the "Karl Rove of Sonoma County."[27] After moving to Santa Rosa from Sacramento in 1992, he set about building both a profitable consulting business and an exceptionally successful electoral machine.

Williams was initially introduced to the Santa Rosa development community as a consulting pollster for a road tax ballot measure. The job opened doors for contacts with influential community figures and organizations like SCA, the Santa Rosa Chamber of Commerce and local builders' associations. Those relationships enabled him to quickly establish a network of clients for a year-round consulting and lobbying business. His company, Delphi, has prospered with its specialized services in public relations and marketing, government affairs and political campaign consultation.

The business income from his Delphi clients has allowed Williams to develop the box of tools essential for not only any good commercial marketing operation, but also for political campaigning. First and foremost, perhaps, through his surveys and public opinion polls, he collects data critical to winning strategies for marketing, passing ballot measures and electing candidates to public office. He knows who's who in the media, has extensive sources for marketing materials and is able to plan and reserve media advertising space months in advance.

HERB WILLIAMS CAMPAIGN MANAGER FOR PRO-DEVELOPER SLATES

Herb Williams moved to Santa Rosa in 1992, setting up a business consulting service. "In Sonoma County, he has run 31 successful campaigns for 19 City Council Members and two County Supervisors, defeated a recall campaign in Rohnert Park, passed Measure O, a quarter percent sales tax for police, fire and gang prevention in Santa Rosa and passed Measure A which banned fireworks in Santa Rosa. He was instrumental in the designation of Memorial Hospital as the Trauma Center for Sonoma County." (quoted from Williams's Delphi company website)

Williams draws on his business apparatus to produce polls and make media arrangements backing up his work as campaign manager for growth machine slates, sometimes charging his candidate clients "only nominal sums, between $1 and $1,000." His dual role in politics and business "has raised concerns about the influence Williams wields." For example, he was a lead negotiator for the multi-million dollar city trash-hauling franchise, extended in 2010 by a City Council with three members whose campaigns Williams managed. (quote from McCoy, "Power Player" 2005)

Williams' polling capabilities provide his candidates with a tremendous advantage. As a Press Democrat article of April 2005 noted, "(It is)18 months from the next statewide elections and Herb Williams is already busy polling voters…he'll have the information ready for the campaigns he chooses to manage for the November 2006 elections."[28] No other political consultant or candidate in Santa Rosa comes close to matching the extent of polling information available to slates managed by Williams. Critics contend that the cost of such polls is at least partially underwritten by those who also support his chosen election candidates, and the true value never shows up on campaign finance reports

The synergy between Williams, his business clients and SCA lies at the heart of the electoral machine. Press Democrat political reporter Mike McCoy in his definitive 2005 biographic piece portraying Williams, [29] took note of "criticism that his candidates are tied too closely to business interests and suspicions that lucrative private consulting contracts give him a financial advantage in developing election strategies." Williams, McCoy reported, provides his services to some candidates for only nominal costs – as low as a token $1 – to manage their campaigns.

FOLLOWING THE MONEY

Follow the money, they say in politics, and the trail from growth machine slate candidates in Santa Rosa races leads not surprisingly to local developers, financiers and construction industry executives. They are the same interests that support SCA and campaigns of candidates managed by Herb Williams. Much, if not all, of the past money flow can be tracked on campaign finance reports (Forms 460), required by California law and maintained by the City Clerk, who now also posts them on the city website. Press Democrat reporters, to their great credit, have regularly written articles on the major trends.

The following quotes, taken from various Press Democrat articles, document campaign contributions to growth machine candidates:

--"In the about three weeks (before election day 2000) the four candidates supported by the building industry received a total of nearly $100,000 in contributions."

-- (in 2002) "the bulk of Blanchard's cash came from the real estate and development communities which also were heavy contributors to Condron and Sawyer."... "Among the largest contributors were the owners and family members of Mead Clark Lumber and Cobblestone Homes, which distributed contributions of $17,820 and $14,500, respectively in nearly equal amounts to Blanchard, Condron and Sawyer." (The three mentioned names were the three pro-developer candidates running that year with Williams.)

--(in 2004) "Sawyer's largest contributors included developers Larry Wasem and Borue O'Brien and Cobblestone Homes."... "Pierce's largest contributors include several developers"... "(Bender's) largest contributors include developer Alan Strachan, Veale Investments .." (Martini's) "major supporters also come mainly from the development and real estate community and include Ken C. Martin, Wasem, O'Brien, Strachan, Cobblestone Homes, Veale Investments, and Air Center West owner Woodrow Erstad." (These four candidates comprised the Williams slate that year.)

--(in 2006) "the Coalition for a Better Sonoma County points to records showing that 65 percent of Poulsen's campaign money and 84 percent of Faber's came from development related business." (The campaigns of Poulsen and Faber along with that of Blanchard were managed by Williams that year.)

-- (in 2008) "All five (Williams-managed slate members) received contributions from a host of business and building-related groups. They include the North Bay Leadership Council, California Real Estate PAC, Mead Clark owner Kevin Destruel and EMS Management. (Four of the slate) also received contributions from the Sonoma County Alliance."

The concentration of large sums from a relatively few individuals and organizations is noteworthy. Although as detailed in succeeding chapters, progressive and independent candidates have at times raised comparable sums, they are heavily dependent on small individual contributors. They have relatively few large donors, comprising a wealthy friend or two and at times a labor union with a large membership base. By contrast, as indicated above, the wealth of land-based interests tends to produce contributions from a small number of rich individuals who stand to profit personally from pro-developer City Council decisions on land use.

In Santa Rosa as elsewhere, the practice of "bundling" often appears to amplify individual contributions. The Santa Rosa limit is $500 from any one person for contribution to one candidate. One can argue of course that married couples have similar interests so it shouldn't be unexpected to have "housewives" show up, as they often do, on lists of contributors, but in many cases, there seems a clearly marked loophole effect. An example of a "bundle" that shows unusual family unity can be found on Jane Bender's Form 460 of December 31, 2004, which lists the maximum $500 contribution each from: 1) developer William Gallaher, 2) housewife Cynthia Gallaher, 3) construction supervisor Steven Gallaher, 4) student Nicole Gallaher, 5) student Molly Gallaher, 6) secretary Joan Gallaher and 7) retired Patrick Gallaher.

THE CAMPAIGN PACKAGE FOR CANDIDATES

But money is only a part of the package. Progressive candidate David Rosas gave a penetrating view[30] of the broader resource deficit facing a candidate like himself who was not on a Williams slate, had no substantial personal funds of his own available, and depended on grassroots community support. When Rosas ran for City Council in 2008, there were two other Latinos on Santa Rosa ballots. He was not competing directly against the other two, but all three were in a 'diversity' spotlight since no Latino had ever been elected to either the City Council or the County Board of Supervisors. After the election dust settled, Rosas penned an op-ed piece for the Press Democrat comparing his losing effort with the winning results obtained by his two colleagues, Council candidate Ernesto Olivares and Supervisor candidate Efren Carrillo, who both ran with strong developer support under the Williams umbrella.

Olivares and Carrillo, Rosas wrote, "did not have to worry about the little things as I did because they had a campaign consultant and adequate funding from their donors. This is an important lesson in a citywide or county election; a campaign consultant and buckets of money are necessary. They also aligned themselves with business interests that provided resources and expertise." Williams of course is much more than a "campaign consultant," being able not only to advise, but also to open funding taps, provide polling data, and secure sites for signs, ad placements and organizational as well as individual endorsements.

All three of the Latino candidates had full-time jobs when they ran, but as Rosas noted, "being a candidate is a full-time endeavor. Raising money is the No. 1 priority. Money, money, money is the mother's milk of a campaign. I needed more milk." Rosas' point about how money is supplied on a silver platter, as it were, to candidates managed by Williams was confirmed by another candidate who had been called and asked to run for the 2008 campaign by Lisa Schaffner, SCA's Executive Director. She promised all necessary funding would be assured if the person would join the Williams slate.[31]

THE PD – FOR PRESS DEMOCRAT AND PRO-DEVELOPER

Santa Rosa's daily newspaper, the Press Democrat, has to be counted as a valuable asset of the pro-developer machine. True to Professor Domhoff's predictive analysis, quoted in Chapter 4, the PD is a daily that invariably supports the local growth coalition, but at the same time plays a "statesman-like" and flexible role, consistent with its need to appeal to a diverse constituency of readers. In recent elections, the PD, for example, has not endorsed every candidate on the pro-developer slate for City Council – in 2006, the paper backed two of three from the slate and one from among opposing progressives, and in 2008, it endorsed three of five from the slate plus two from the progressive side. In the 2008 County Supervisor races, however, the PD did endorse all three pro-developer candidates and vigorously supported them.

Critics assert that the Press Democrat in fact gives important support to all pro-developer candidates through its editorial policy and allegedly biased news coverage. More blatant examples of unfair editorializing at election time include a vituperative attack in 2002 on progressive candidate Marsha Vas Dupre for publicizing factual information on sources of contributions made to pro-developer candidates. Although Dupre's information was accurate and a matter of public record, the PD slammed her for being "divisive." For another example, at the start of the 2008 campaign when progressives made an early joint endorsement of three candidates, a PD "gotcha" editorial knocked them for alleged lack of diversity, but the paper failed to note that one of the candidates concerned, Michael Allen, has a Latino mother. And in 2008, PD editorial writers waxed eloquent about the evils of labor union contributions to progressive candidates, but said little or nothing about the special interest developer contributions to the pro-developer slate. Nor does the PD extend its slashing criticism of labor to Santa Rosa public employee unions, whose leaders sit on the Political Action Committee of the Sonoma County Alliance.

As for its news coverage in 2008, progressives would say the Press Democrat showed obvious, even outrageous, bias in the county supervisor races. On the one hand, it printed several stories critical of progressive candidate Rue Furch, calling attention to her failures to pay taxes, while on the other, it said little or nothing about the past record of pro-developer candidate Sharon Wright and the fines levied against her for conflict of interest while serving on the Santa Rosa City Council. And a post-election news story rankled progressives with its lead assertions that union and environmental groups outspent business and development "coalitions," when in fact numbers buried deeper in the story showed that direct contributions to the Wright campaign from business and developer interests more than made up any disparity.[32]

That said, the Press Democrat deserves credit for its many news stories which laid bare details of campaign financing and honestly addressed potential conflicts of interest in the murky circles radiating out from City Hall. Reporter McCoy's seminal biographic article on Herb Williams asked the right questions, and on the editorial side, the paper excoriated Mike Martini for taking the job as SCA Executive Director while still Mayor of Santa Rosa. It also commendably prints letters from all quarters and opens its op-ed page to views with which the paper disagrees.

The relevant point here, however, is that the Press Democrat year-in, year-out aids and abets the pro-developer political machine. It is not, of course, a crime by any stretch of the imagination to be pro-developer, or to use the editorial page to advance that view, or to have the publisher be a leader in the Chamber of Commerce. But it does add up to an important pillar of the growth coalition, and in political terms, greatly helps stack the deck against progressives in election years.

LOOKING TO COME BACK

Despite the considerable resources assembled by the pro-developer machine in 2006 and 2008, it lost its City Council majority to progressives. The analysis in Chapter 2 suggests that the flagging of pro-developer fortunes was due in large measure to rising citizen concerns over both environmental protection and undue developer influence in city politics. Put another way, the pro-growth ideology, which had so long propelled the machine's success, had finally been overtaken by new realities.

On the ground, the stalling of grandiose downtown plans and the City's budget crisis may well have cost the machine votes. The failure of highly-touted high-rise building projects had an aura of bad planning and wasted energy, offsetting the promotion of local business and nightlife. While Council Members in power from 2006-08 could hardly be blamed for the national recession that hammered the City budget, there was a certain validity to perceptions that they had long promoted growth too heavily, overspent, and failed to act in timely fashion when the difficulties began to unfold.

The machine was also diminished by the loss of its energetic and highly visible leader on the Council, Bob Blanchard. Coming on the heels of Martini's unexpected resignation and the eve of Bender's retirement, that left only heir-apparent Sawyer on the first team. Bender's decision to run for the remainder of Blanchard's term virtually assured the machine of two seats, but four were needed to gain the majority. Olivares ran well to secure the third seat for The Team, but neither of the remaining slate members came close to winning the requisite fourth slot.

In losing, however, the pro-developer machine remained a formidable force. It commands the elements necessary for running campaigns that can win – organization, business elite allies, and campaign expertise. What seems to have tipped it out of office more than anything else was the weakening of its appeal to voters, and on that count, it started in 2008 to reinvent or repackage itself by trying to distance its candidates from "special interests" and align more closely with environmental protection in voters' eyes. The Williams polling operation will doubtless point the way to improving its image for future campaigns. With the Press Democrat's evident though perhaps unwitting assistance, the growth machine by mid-2009 had already manifested a strategy for 2010 of trying to brand the progressive majority as "anti-business."

Can the progressives stave off a growth machine resurgence? It will not be easy to do so, since they are short on the central organizational strength and financial backing enjoyed by the developer-backed machine. The next two chapters take up the theory and practice of progressive coalition building.

CHAPTER 6

PROGRESSIVE MOVEMENTS AND TAKING ON GROWTH MACHINES

The 2008 progressive victory was exceptional but hardly a fluke – environmental, neighborhood and social justice advocates have long been forces to be reckoned with in Santa Rosa and Sonoma County. They regularly challenged the pro-developer City Councils in Santa Rosa through the 1980s and 1990s, and managed significant advances most notably perhaps on environmental protection issues, including enactment of Urban Growth Boundaries.

From the 1950s on, Sonoma County activists stood with the leading edge of conservation, environmental protection and open space movements. The same cannot be said of Santa Rosa itself, where sprawling development held sway through the late 1980s before it was slowed, if not halted, by growth limitation measures passed in the early 1990s. Santa Rosa progressives won a number of important battles over the last two decades, although until 2008 they kept losing the war to decisively reorder city priorities on matters of concern to them.

Most progressive organizations in Santa Rosa are issue-oriented. They can be very effective when lobbying for their particular objectives, but hard to pull together when it comes to marshalling forces for city-wide elections. That is not unique to Santa Rosa.

This chapter first provides an overview of the dynamics of progressive urban politics in America, and then describes the local base from which progressive candidates draw support for City Council campaigns. The next chapter will take a look at how Santa Rosa progressives hope to mobilize more effectively for upcoming elections and sustain their hard-won political momentum.

THE POLITICS OF PLACE[33]

Nation-wide, two of the strongest sources of opposition to growth machines have been environmentalists and, especially in larger cities, neighborhood residents facing social injustice and degradation of urban centers. There are numerous examples of successful progressive "revolts" in both large and small municipalities, in the latter case often led by university faculty and students as happened close to home in Berkeley, Palo Alto and Santa Cruz – the success of progressives in Santa Cruz, who have held City Council power there since 1981, was described in *The Leftmost City*, published in 2009. In other locales, retirement communities and the tourist industry have found common cause with "enviros" to resist industrial developments such as oil refineries that can pose threats to lifestyles, economic well-being or open space and local habitat conservation efforts.

For large cities, San Francisco became a model of the progressive way. In its case, neighborhood empowerment was perhaps the single strongest theme that kept progressives in power and imposed conditions on growth. Setting their sights on better parks, schools, affordable housing and neighborhood empowerment, San Francisco progressives mounted successful drives to curtail big development projects and/or obtain substantial "linkage" funding for quality of life investments. These developments produced a major academic study, captured in a 1992 book titled *Left Coast City*.

It is, however, still hard sledding for progressives in most places to prevail against the siren song of continuous growth. Despite the increasing realization that Americans need to change their ways, powerful developer interests and like-minded allies continue to promote the pro-growth ideology and development patterns that brought prosperity and personal independence to millions of Americans in the last half century. That was then, of course, but even now, outright rejection of major development projects can still be problematic except in extreme cases, so progressives frequently find themselves obliged to limit their goals and negotiate for lesser concessions or tradeoffs.[34]

Nonetheless, alternative strategies for growth have made notable progress in recent years. It is becoming more evident to more people that high-rise office buildings, high impact shopping centers and large scale suburban housing projects rarely pay their full cost share for the burdens their added presence imposes on water supply, transportation systems, schools, and other public services. San Francisco was among the first municipalities to seek redress when in 1985 it levied five distinct fees on new office construction to support transit, child care, housing, open space and public art. Other cities have since followed suit and in some places development impact fees are now the most important method for financing new infrastructure.

For smaller California municipalities such as Santa Rosa, however, impact fees can be a double-edged sword. In the wake of Proposition 13, cities scrambling to maintain adequate revenue sources often are desperate to attract new development, in particular big box stores and large-scale shopping centers. Fearing to lose projects to competitor jurisdictions, City Councils may reduce or forego impact fees as an incentive – or even subsidize projects as Santa Rosa did by advancing $3 million to sweeten the pot for the Santa Rosa Marketplace shopping center development on Santa Rosa Avenue.

Chapter 11 will return to the difficulties of California municipal financing, which has become a problem of crisis proportions for cities such as Santa Rosa. California's special case aside, there are significant downsides to the practice of negotiating off-sets as justification for continuous growth, rather than trying to reshape the nature of the growth itself. Competition between local governments for sales tax revenues tends to fragment metropolitan areas and increase disparities between have and have-not districts within a city or between tax jurisdictions, while pitting city against city to discourage a more sensible regional approach.

Financing is of course critical to City government, but it is not the only consideration. It is important also to sustain the environment and quality of life for city residents. In general, progressives look to development frameworks inspired by the New Urbanism and Smart Growth movements for balanced approaches to meet these requirements as well as to generate economic activity.

With regard to development policy, labor unions have also begun to focus on quality of life and sustainability issues for their members. Labor interests often overlap with progressives on matters like local hiring, living wage and affordable housing. Unions in recent years have pressed for negotiated agreements on employment issues for large projects, while many developers and builders have fought hard against them. President George W. Bush issued an executive order prohibiting use in federal projects of such negotiations, known as Project Labor Agreement (PLAs), but President Obama reversed the policy and encouraged PLAs soon after he took office. The topic surged to

> PROGRESSIVE ADVOCACY:
> KEY POLITICALLY ACTIVE
> ORGANIZATIONS
>
> Progressive political advocacy
> Concerned Citizens for Santa Rosa
> Coalition for a Better Sonoma County
>
> Environmental sustainability & planning
> Accountable Development Coalition
> Sierra Club – Sonoma Group
> Sonoma County Conservation Action
> Green Belt Alliance – Sonoma/Marin
> Sonoma County Bicycle Coalition
> Sonoma County Transportation and
> Land-use Coalition
> Sonoma County Water Coalition
> Various neighborhood associations
>
> Social justice
> Housing Advocacy Group
> Living Wage Coalition
>
> Labor unions (Sonoma County Locals)
> Service Employees (SEIU)
> Electrical Workers (IBEW)
> North Bay Labor Council
>
> Democratic Party organizations/clubs

the fore in Santa Rosa in 2009 when Keith Woods of the North Coast Builders Exchange bitterly attacked local labor and progressive allies for pursuing community benefit agreements (CBAs), which typically include PLA features along with questions of impacts on the surrounding community. Editorialists at the Press Democrat essentially agreed with Woods, but some key developers remained supportive of CBAs for the advantages to them of predictability, good labor relations on the job and neighborhood support.

CONSERVATION AND ANTI-SPRAWL MOVEMENTS

In Sonoma County, grassroots organizations took up the cudgels over half a century ago to conserve and protect land resources. Following northern California Sierra Club traditions, Petalumans Bill and Lucy Kortum with a host of like-minded environmentalists successfully prevented the building of a nuclear power plant at Bodega Bay and later helped secure public access to California's coastline. In the 1970s, a group of private citizens in Sonoma Valley formed the Sonoma Land Trust to promote land conservation and develop strategies for private and public efforts to achieve this goal. It subsequently expanded its area of interest to include all of Sonoma County – to date it has protected more than 19,000 acres of scenic, agricultural and open lands from the Baylands along Highway 37 to north of the Russian River.

But the environmental movement was much slower to affect Santa Rosa itself. Hewlett-Packard's 1970s move to locate a high-tech campus in the Fountaingrove Ranch area brought an early manifestation of citizen concern over environmental impacts, and as Gaye Lebaron recounts,[35] initial planning meetings were packed with neighbors full of questions about what was foreseen for the hillsides and ridge tops. But interest petered out, and later development expanded inexorably up and over the hilltops despite protective ordinances. In the late 1970s, citizens opposed to a highway bridge over Spring Lake Park came out in force and killed the project before funding became available, but overall development continued to boom into the 1980s, with almost no restriction.

The ongoing rush of housing permits and a series of major sewage spills spurred concerns over both urban sprawl and the political power of pro-growth elites. Santa Rosa lawyer Dick Day was among the first to recognize that progressives needed more unity and stronger focus on political action to compete with the growth coalition. Although developer interests had formed the Sonoma County Alliance as a political lobbying group in 1974, it wasn't until twelve years later that Day and others organized Concerned Citizens for Santa Rosa (CCSR). One of Day's allies, Guy Connor coordinated a town hall-type meeting in a local church to get the ball rolling.

Five years later, in 1991, Day teamed up with Bill Kortum, Joan Vilms and Juliana Doms to found Sonoma County Conservation Action (SCCA), to work on a county-wide basis. SCCA set itself up as a grassroots organization with the "mission to better our quality of life in Sonoma County for all generations, through educating and directly engaging the public on local environmental issues and policies."[36] Both CCSR and SCCA recognized that political action, as opposed to narrow issue advocacy, was necessary to change the course set by entrenched pro-growth coalitions in the county and its cities.

Building on solid popular support, at the turn of the 1990s progressives mounted successful drives to further protect green space and slow, if not halt, Santa Rosa's urban sprawl. In 1990 a ballot measure limited expansion of the City's urban growth boundary (UGB), which voters six years later revised and extended for a 20-year period. In 1990 voters created the Sonoma County Agricultural Preservation and Open Space District, one of the first such entities established in the country, and financed it through a ¼ % sales tax. In 1992 a Growth Management Ordinance was passed – a survey of citizen attitudes at the time showed nearly 70% were dissatisfied with the city's rapid growth rate. Popular approval also ensured the slow but steady advance through the 1990s of the Prince Greenway creek-side park, championed by City Council Member Steve Rabinowitsh, who worked tirelessly with other progressives on the Council for greater attention to conservation of natural resources as well as promotion of the arts in downtown.

The growth control and open space measures were, however, only partial solutions. They limit the ultimate extent of development and to some degree its pace, but sympathetic City Councils can still provide exceptions from a range of growth constraints or promote infill by large projects. Environmental and open space issues still on the progressive agenda for coming years include strengthening of green building ordinances, further protection of hillsides and ridge tops, adequacy and location of parks and recreation facilities, protection of historic landmarks, and extension of alternative transportation.

DIVERSITY AND SOCIAL JUSTICE MOVEMENTS

A second major objective of Santa Rosa progressive activism in the 1990s was to open up city government. The focus of the effort was, to again borrow a turn of phrase from Chris Coursey, "the glaring homogeneity of the City Council."[37] Through the 1980s and 1990s the vast majority of Council members came from the city's wealthy, white northeast suburbs. In response to persistent pressure, citizen commissions were formed to consider City Charter amendments for district elections, expansion of boards and commissions and more neighborhood involvement in city government.

Pro-developer City Council majorities steadfastly blocked the potentially most significant measure, district elections. In its basic form, the idea is to have City Council members elected each from a limited district rather than on a city-wide ballot, and proposals for such a system in Santa Rosa were directed in particular at assuring participation for the city's large and growing Latino community – a political "sleeping giant," poorly integrated and under-represented in the city's political power structure. The pro-developer political machine has a powerful underlying interest to retain city-wide elections where it has an advantage with its greater ability to fund expensive mailers and advertisements that must reach all of the city's 70,000-plus registered voters.

Efforts to introduce limited measures to enable community involvement fared slightly better in the face of stolid Council opposition. In 2002, a ballot measure that carried with a 60% voter approval led to adoption of language now in the City Charter calling for measures "to greatly increase citizen and neighborhood participation and responsibility." As an alternative of sorts to District Elections, the same ballot measure also mandated creation of a "District Commission" of citizens to advise the Council. By way of implementing this provision, the Council set up the Citizens Advisory Board (CAB), but gave it no significant resources or role other than to administer small neighborhood grants for local improvement. The CAB appointed after the 2008 elections took a more pro-active approach to fulfilling the Charter language, established a closer working relationship with the Council and as of 2010 was reviewing its role and duties.

Absent an effective official channel, neighborhood associations individually lobbied the City for attention to their interests. The West End under Carol Dean had impressive success in fighting urban blight and absentee landlord neglect. In Southwest and Roseland, the Southwest Area Citizens' Group with a longish history of activism was later paralleled by newer neighborhood associations around McMinn and Hughes Avenues, centered on Roseland's particular set of issues as a County-governed hole surrounded by a City-governed donut.

Historic preservation also surged to the fore in the early 1990s. Several districts in the older parts of Santa Rosa around the town's center achieved designation as Historic Districts, when residents pressed to preserve the ambiance of their neighborhoods against the potential encroachment of commercial development. However, numerous individual landlords and pro-growth interests successfully worked to keep historic protections limited, such that the downtown, including 4th Street, and stretches of Mendocino and College Avenues were excluded primarily because property owners wanted to have flexibility for commercial development.

On a somewhat different track to advance progressive interests, Arnold Sternberg founded the Housing Advocacy Group in 1998 to push for stronger action throughout the county on housing for lower income groups. Its counsel and current leader, David Grabill, proved a forceful advocate, successfully suing four jurisdictions, including Santa Rosa to require more effective affordable housing policies. Pro-developer interests criticized Grabill as being too uncompromising – for example when City Council Member Janet Condron said "I gag at paying his legal fees" – but there is no denying that lower income residents benefited from his success.[38]

THE PROGRESSIVE POLITICAL BASE IN 2010

In broad terms, there is a veritable army of progressive activists and organizations in Santa Rosa. The exceptional array of advocates within the city and county covers the full range of progressive issues: gender, race, religious, and age equality, protection for children, human rights, victims of crime and abuse; help for the poor, the ill and the homeless; promotion of health and equity for the disadvantaged; the peace movement and more too numerous to list here. By far the great majority of the area's progressives, however, devote their energy to their immediate causes, and leave to others the political work of City Council elections.

This book is concerned more narrowly with how progressive aspirations translate into political support for candidates and members of

Santa Rosa's City Council. A brief overview of the key organizations that emerged from past years of advocacy to carry forward what has become a grassroots political base follows:

ENVIRONMENTAL ORGANIZATIONS

The Sierra Club remains a centerpiece of environmental activism – its current three-pronged focus carries forward traditional concerns to protect wildlife and habitat, and adds two more recent themes, "smart energy solutions" to promote renewable sources and new technologies, and "safe and healthy communities" to fight pollution of air and water. The Club's Redwood Chapter has 10,000 members and is headquartered in Santa Rosa, which is also the center of its Sonoma Group, the Sonoma County element. The Club still concentrates much of its energy on conservation of our wilderness, forests and water, but for some years now has also given priority to climate change and urban issues, along with a Political Committee to endorse candidates and support ballot measures.

Santa Rosa Council Member Veronica Jacobi has been an active Sierra Club participant and is a director on the Sonoma Group Executive Committee. The Sonoma Group Chair, Steve Birdlebough, provides another bridge into Santa Rosa progressive politics through his activities

---

STEVE RABINOWITSH CITY COUNCIL MEMBER 1998–2006

Popular and hard-working during his 8 years on the Council, Steve Rabinowitsh always found himself in the progressive minority, but he proved an exceptionally effective champion of his chosen causes. He was a co-founder of the Committee for Restoring Santa Rosa Creek and led the effort to create the Prince Memorial Greenway, which rehabilitated the creek for trout, created a vibrant park system and expanded bikeway links. Rabinowitsh also helped energize the Open Space District, was the prime Council mover in making arts a prominent feature of downtown development, and worked to bring the SMART rail project to fruition.

While on the Council, Rabinowitsh was known as a team player. If competence and popularity were the criteria for Mayoral duties, Rabinowitsh would have held the office for a term or more, but during his time, the growth machine majority never relaxed its grip on control of Council operations and agenda. He teaches political science at the Santa Rosa Junior College, and has remained a civic activist, concentrating on environmental protections and promotion of the arts.

with local community groups and advocacy for the SMART train project.

The Greenbelt Alliance for Sonoma and Marin Counties is also a substantial regional presence and influential non-profit, lobbying in Sonoma County on a range of environmental issues. From its main office in San Francisco, the Alliance opened a northern branch in 1995 to help lead the way for establishing Urban Growth Boundaries. Its branch Director, Amanda Bornstein, and her popular predecessor, Daisy Pistey-Lyhne, have been familiar figures in city progressive circles, as the Alliance joined with like-minded groups in Santa Rosa on such issues as the City's General Plan, affordable housing, transit planning, and UGB renewal, among others. The Alliance promotes or opposes specific development projects, but has not explicitly endorsed political candidates.

Two increasingly urgent issues – water and transportation – have spawned numerous local organizations with considerable expertise to promote sustainability in these areas and keep a watchful eye on local government policy-making. Water has remained a "hot button" issue, given that many Santa Rosans are skeptical of supply projections and the impact of global warming. The non-profit Sonoma County Water Coalition (SCWC) has 30 participating organizations, claiming to represent more than 24,000 voters, and works hard to influence elected officials.

Among the Water Coalition's members that focus strictly on water concerns, a few have directly lobbied local government. Most vocal perhaps has been the Russian River Watershed Protection Committee, chaired by Brenda Adelman. The testimony and commentaries from Adelman and her colleagues are typically based on in-depth and informed analysis, such that government agencies give them serious consideration. Other organizations in SCWC are less politically active, directing their energies more into conservation projects and public education.

In the transportation sphere, the Sonoma County Transportation and Land-Use Coalition (SCTLC) was founded in the early 1990s to pull together environmentalists interested in the special characteristics of transportation issues. Unlike the SC Water Coalition, it relies more on individuals than on participating organizations, but it coordinates closely with several, in particular the Sierra Club, Greenbelt Alliance and of course the SMART rail project along with regional and local government agencies. SCTLC has been registered as a Political Action Committee since 1992, and has become a respected "adviser" to local authorities, even when it expresses strong opposition to official policy proposals.

The foregoing "base" of environmental activism in Santa Rosa and Sonoma County spans a wide range of individuals, including many strong supporters of the pro-developer political faction. As mentioned in the first chapter of this book, one has to guard against stereotyping "environmentalists" as anti-development. Nonetheless, in political terms, the interests and citizen engagement reflected across the environmentalist groups noted above provide the single strongest pillar of the progressive political movement in Santa Rosa.

NEIGHBORHOOD ASSOCIATIONS

Since 2000, Santa Rosa neighborhood advocates have reenergized their political activism. The West End Neighborhood Association and the commercial Railroad Square Historic District next door assumed greater importance as the SMART project evolved. In a different context, the Southwest and Roseland neighborhood associations also took on added dimensions as the City and County sought – unsuccessfully thus far – to facilitate the City's annexation of this large County-administered island within the city limits.

On similar tracks, neighborhood leaders around the downtown area became increasingly restive as infill projects proceed with little attention to the concerns of established residential and historic districts. In 2002, St. Rose Historic District residents objected to features of a large development project on their periphery. Led by Denise Hill, they soon found themselves fighting almost tooth and nail to achieve relatively modest modifications of design and traffic flow. Judy Kennedy and fellow residents in Burbank Gardens along with Karen Macken of Juilliard Park took the city to task over urban design issues, while initial proposals for high-rise buildings in downtown energized Cherry St. and Junior College neighbors who feared commercial encroachment on 7th St. and College Avenue.

Neighborhoods have been spurred to organize themselves by a variety of concerns. Residents in Northwest Santa Rosa under Jack Swearengen tried, with only limited success, to get the city to implement General Plan provisions in connection with new development there. Bennett Valley area residents, led by Julie Combs, Thea Hensel, Jake Bayless, and numerous others, banded together anew, in particular to seek beneficial communal use of the fallow Highway 12 right of way, as well as to build community. Sharon Cisneros pulled Bellevue Ranch area residents together for classic reasons – to help neighbors get to know each other, improve park and police services and generally promote pride of place. In Roseland, Fred Krueger of Hughes Avenue worked with local residents to persuade the city and county to purchase a large undeveloped tract, studded with heritage oaks, for a much needed open-space park – as of early 2010, their hard slogging appeared to be nearing the goal.

One of the most contentious struggles at the neighborhood level involved citizen objections to streetscape features of the new Santa Rosa Junior College parking garage on Mendocino Avenue. College and City administrations essentially ignored neighborhood suggestions for entry design improvements, whereupon nearby residents, led by Jenny Bard, a passionate advocate for attractive walkable/bikeable streetscapes, revitalized the Junior College Neighborhood Association and raised money to bring in national expert Dan Burden. With his help, the neighbors persuasively demonstrated better ways to route autos and accommodate foot and bicycle traffic along the street and sidewalk. The then-relatively new Sonoma County Bicycle Coalition joined the fray with a lawsuit concerning inadequacy of bicycle features, resulting among other points in a commitment by the College to provide $1 million toward a pedestrian/bicycle bridge over Highway 101.

A number of these neighborhood associations joined in late 2005 to form the Neighborhood Alliance of Santa Rosa. The Alliance Charter sets forth a strongly progressive agenda with promotion of livable neighborhoods and citizen engagement at the center. Although several Alliance leaders have been active in political campaigns, the Alliance itself adopted a policy not to endorse candidates, but rather to focus on issues of neighborhood interest, including environmental sustainability, good urban design, citizen engagement and district elections – in 2006 and 2008 the Alliance also sponsored candidates' forums.

LABOR UNIONS

Organized labor has become an important support element for the progressive political movement in Santa Rosa. Although only about 17% of workers in the local area are unionized, the unions have the resources to provide political expertise, continuity, and funding to a greater extent than other progressive organizations which are generally smaller in numbers and typically have little left over after their own grassroots fund raising. By and large, the labor movement espouses liberal causes and therefore in Santa Rosa finds itself aligned with progressive coalitions on many issues.

Unions are, however, widely split with respect to support of progressive candidates for City Council. As noted in Chapter 4, city employee unions have cast their lot with the growth machine, to the extent that leaders of all three main city unions have worked actively through the Sonoma County Alliance to support pro-developer political activities and candidates. Nonetheless, city public safety unions in 2008 endorsed Allen and the Police Officers Association declined to support Olivares, the pro-developer slate candidate who himself was a retired police officer. Such anomalies seem related primarily to personalities rather than political ideologies.

North Bay labor movement leaders like Michael Allen, Lisa Maldonado, Jack Buckhorn,

---

MICHAEL ALLEN
PROGRESSIVE MEDIATOR AND CATALYST

Michael Allen is best known as for his long service as Executive Director of SEIU Local 707 and since 2007, as the Santa Rosa-based District Director for State Senator Pat Wiggins. He is Chair of the SMART Train Citizens Oversight Committee, has recently served on the Santa Rosa Planning Commission, and in 2010 launched his campaign for election to the California State Assembly

Allen is founding member of Solar Sonoma and helped catalyze formation of the Accountable Development Coalition which in late 2009 negotiated the first major local Community Benefit Agreement with developers of Sonoma Mountain Village in Rohnert Park. He is a lawyer, registered nurse and mediator – his distinguished record of work and service includes nine terms as President of the North Bay Labor Council, membership on a Sierra Club Legal Defense Team, and helping to establish the Sonoma County Day Care Center in 1992.

Marty Bennett and Steven Benjamin have advanced labor's role in promoting a "community consensus" for future development. In 2004, interviewed by the Press Democrat, Allen described the need for labor to build partnerships with environmental organizations, neighborhood associations, nonprofit and business groups that support social equity and sustainable development.[39] Adopting this approach, SEIU and allies in the North Bay Labor Council have looked to work more closely with progressive coalitions.

THE DEMOCRATIC PARTY

Santa Rosa's Democratic State Legislators Noreen Evans and Pat Wiggins both built influential personal, as opposed to political party, networks in Santa Rosa during the 1990s when they won election to the City Council. Come election time in the city, Evans and Wiggins are still widely perceived as progressive leaders of the local community rather than Democratic Party figures when they engage in City Council campaigns by endorsing candidates, hosting fund-raisers, and making personal appearances. Their endorsements in local campaigns are if anything more important to help candidates with name-recognition and fund raising than to give them the political stamp of Democrats in an area where Republicans have become barely visible.

Only recently have local Democratic Party organs and officers begun to throw real weight into City Council campaigns. 2008 marked the escalation point, although it was of course an unusual year as Obama-mania swept through Sonoma County. Young Democrats and Progressive Democrats raised their voices not so much within, but alongside the main Democratic Party establishment, which is itself divided by history into the two components of a Central Committee and a Democratic Club. The two are separate organizations, but have moved closer together in recent years.

In 2008 Stephen Gale took over as Chair of the Central Committee and pulled it together after a period of internal factionalism. Gale and longtime Santa Rosa Democratic Club leader Liz Basile made a point of going to bat for progressive City Council candidates. In general, however, Democratic voters have looked more to issues for guidance than to the Party label since the majority of candidates, whether pro-developer or progressive in Santa Rosa are registered Democrats. As is the case noted above with Evans and Wiggins, engagement in City Council campaigns by local Democratic Party office holders tends to follow personal networking with friends and progressive associates.

INDEPENDENT PROGRESSIVES

There are in Santa Rosa politically active progressives who have their own priorities and work primarily as individuals or through an independent organization. The best known and arguably most influential across the board is Susan Moore, who heads up the No Name Women's Group, a formidable assembly of women from across the county working together on issues of common interest. Moore also is an effective fundraiser on her own, and many leading progressives have been graced one time or another with a campaign kickoff or a fundraiser at her home.

A determined and energetic community activist, Moore has also mounted major efforts for education of underprivileged girls, and recently became the sparkplug for community support of Roseland University Prep (RUP). A small charter public high school, RUP quickly built an extraordinary record of inspiring high academic performance on the part of its students, the great majority of whom come from Latino and other minorities. Although Moore has diverged from some of her progressive colleagues with her vigorous support for the proposed Graton Rancheria Casino, that has not noticeably diminished the influence that comes from her devotion to other exemplary causes, her broad network of contacts, and her productive fundraisers.

An independent progressive of a completely different type is Geoff Johnson, a relatively solitary figure who has operated on the sidelines of organized political activity. Johnson made his Santa Rosam political mark as a vigilant watchdog for California's Fair Political Practices Commission (FPPC) and for enforcement of the State's Brown Act, which requires transparency in local government. He helped expose City Administration efforts to "sneak by" a $3 million subsidy for the Santa Rosa Marketplace project on Santa Rosa Avenue, and he blew the whistle on conflicts of interest involving two City Council Members and a Planning Commissioner. The Marketplace revelation led to a successful Sierra Club suit against the developers and the City, while in the other cases, the FPPC levied stiff fines against three growth machine proponents, Council Members Sharon Wright and Janet Condron, and

Planning Commissioner Richard Carlile, principal of a Santa Rosa engineering, design and planning firm.

A COALITION DOES NOT A MACHINE MAKE

Pluralism is the nature of the progressive beast. When election time rolls around for City Council, there is no clear progressive quarterback, no over-arching organization and no central banker to pull the energy and resources smoothly together. Past efforts to match the growth machine on these counts have fallen short – as chronicled in the opening chapters of this book, the progressive victory in 2008 came about in part because of strengthened organizational and funding efforts, but also owed much to the inspiration of Obama-mania and new trends in voter perceptions.

Still, progressives deserve credit for trying harder. CCSR from its inception made a point of seeking out capable progressive candidates for City Council, encouraging them to run and supporting their campaigns. SCCA also had a strong political dimension from the beginning. The support of CCSR and SCCA helped several candidates to win City Council seats through the 1990s, notably Pat Wiggins, Noreen Evans, Marsha Vas Dupre, and Steve Rabinowitsh. Wiggins went on to become a State Assembly Member and then a Senator, while Evans followed Wiggins to replace her in the Assembly, and is a candidate to move on to the Senate in 2010 in the wake of Wiggins' retirement after one term.

Unable through the 1990s to secure the brass ring of a City Council majority, progressive leaders redoubled their efforts to form broader political action groups and coalitions. They built on the existing core with CCSR and SCCA, and forged stronger links between labor unions, neighborhood associations, and social justice advocates.

The progressive effort finally paid off in 2008. But can the coalition hold together? The next chapter describes the current make-up of the progressive coalition that powered its way to the 2008 victory and is re-forming for 2010. How does it work if nobody is in charge, and where does the money come from? And at the top of the agenda, can it win two in a row?

CHAPTER 7

PROGRESSIVE COALITION – SANTA ROSA STYLE

The formula for progressive success in Santa Rosa is deceptively simple: combine the broad popular appeal of the progressive message with grassroots organizational support, adequate funding and campaign smarts. Using these elements, Santa Rosa progressives in recent years have constructed a still loose, but increasingly effective political apparatus. The effort bore fruit in 2008.

As indicated in the previous chapter, however, underneath it all progressives in Santa Rosa are a disparate bunch. It is no easy matter to hold coalitions together and re-infuse them with energy each time an election rolls around. Progressive leaders understand this and continue to work on organizational continuity, campaign leadership, money, alliances within the community, and a common articulation of progressive ideals to build voter appeal while combating the distortions of growth ideology and boosterism.

This chapter analyzes how progressives are going about the job of political organization and how well they are doing. It concludes by asking the questions that bear on election cycles in the near future: What should progressives be doing to both govern effectively and sustain their political momentum?

THE PROGRESSIVE TROIKA

In a city where most people are registered Democrats and self-proclaimed liberals, how does one know who the "real" progressive candidates are? As mentioned in Chapter 1, most politically active Santa Rosans, including *Press Democrat* reporters, see City Council election campaigns as three-way contests, pitting a pro-developer slate vs. a progressive group vs. one or more independents. Even before 2008, the pro-developer slate was readily identifiable, but progressives, lacking a "command central" have run individually separate campaigns that may or may not have overlapped. Given such individualized campaign approaches, one has to look to the pattern of support to sort out the core of progressive political activists from the broader group of progressive individuals and organizations discussed in the previous chapter.

By that light, the "official" progressive political label is conferred in the first instance by the endorsements of three key organizations: Sonoma County Conservation Action (SCCA), Concerned Citizens for Santa Rosa (CCSR) and the Coalition for a Better Sonoma County (CBSC). All three have avowedly political missions to advance progressive goals and candidates who support them – together they are a kind of political troika that helps to pull its selected group of progressives down the campaign road.

SCCA is today the most substantial of the three. It has permanent staff to carry out its mission, which at heart is to pursue environmental protection through political action. Its website states its goal as "to better our quality of life in Sonoma County for all generations, through educating and directly engaging the public on local environmental issues and policies." (website at www.conservationaction.org)

Former Mayor and pro-developer Council Member Mike Martini, described SCCA's election role this way: "There are two ways to work a campaign in this community. One is grass roots, like Conservation Action. Their candidates rarely report a whole lot of campaign donations, but they have a lot of worker bees to walk the precincts for them," Martini said. "The other side is those who will not walk a precinct or lick stamps for you but are willing to write you a check."[40]

Four of SCCA's ten Board members (2009) are identified with Santa Rosa: Guy Conner, Marty Bennett, Don Lollock and Ken Wells. The remaining Board members come from other corners of the County, and all have strong environmental protection credentials, most notably, Sonoma County's 'grand old man' of the environmental movement, retired Petaluma veterinarian Bill Kortum, himself a founding member of SCCA. There is considerable networking with other progressive groups: for example, political consultant Guy Connor is active in both CCSR and CBSC; and SRJC Professor Marty Bennett is also a labor union leader and Co-Chair of the Living Wage Coalition.

Grassroots activism is central to SCCA's mission. The SCCA staff, led by its young and vigorous Executive Director Dennis Rosatti, features a robust canvassing component, mounts public information events, keeps a "report card" on the performance of local legislators, promotes local government policies to protect the environment and works aggressively in support of ballot measures and candidates it favors. Until recent financial pressures forced consolidation, the SCCA maintained a Political Action Committee (PAC) with Sebastopol City Council Member Craig Litwin as Political Director to help mobilize progressive political forces.

SCCA's annual Report Card rates both City Council members and County Supervisors. It assigns letter grades from A+ to F for each individual office holder in two categories: "Environmental Voting" and "Listens to Citizens," along with a brief commentary on the individual's performance. For Santa Rosa 2008/09, of those elected on the growth machine slate, Bender, Olivares and Sawyer all received Ds or D+s for their records on environmental voting and listening to voters. Progressive members Wysocky and Jacobi received As or A+s, while Gorin and Dupre were awarded B+s in both categories.

SCCA's stock in trade is the direct political canvassing mentioned above by Mike Martini. Its staff includes a small but accomplished stable of fund raisers and canvass managers for both phone and field activities. SCCA's capabilities have been amplified by addition of a Know Your Neighbor (KYN) program, which since 2004 has been building neighborhood-based teams of residents to meet with their neighbors for discussion of issues and candidates.

CCSR, the second troika member, keys its mission less directly to environmental protection and more to the objective of promoting open, representative and responsive government. To accomplish the goal,

CCSR (www.concernedcitizensforsantarosa.com) sets itself the tasks of "identifying, endorsing and supporting candidates who support our goals; and ...making our voice heard in support of policy that fulfills our mission."

The current (2010) Chair of CCSR is Anne Seeley. She makes a special point of personally attending Santa Rosa City Council meetings to both monitor Council proceedings and rise whenever appropriate to express CCSR's views. Council Members Susan Gorin and Marsha Vas Dupre have served on the CCSR Board – 2010 members include political consultants Guy Connor and Terry Price, SR School Board Member Larry Haenel, lawyer Rick Meechan, Nancy Richards of the League of Women Voters, Beth Martinez and this book's author. Meechan, Connor and Price are also active in the Coalition for a Better Sonoma County.

CCSR today functions primarily as a progressive lobbying and fundraising entity. It does not have staff or a grassroots organizational capability, although its Board and a number of its rank and file participate extensively in election campaigns, working for example on the steering committees of progressive candidates and sometimes walking precincts. CCSR endorses candidates, contributes directly to their campaign war chests and helps to fund independent expenditures (IE) in support of progressive candidates or causes.

| ANNE SEELEY |
| PROGRESSIVE STALWART |

Anne Seeley has been a linchpin of the Santa Rosa progressive movement since Dick Day and a stellar group of like-minded individuals launched CCSR in 1986 to give it a strong political arm. As long-time Chair of the CCSR Board of Directors, she has been a tireless advocate for open and representative government as well as an informal but essential coordinator to promote cooperation among politically active progressive organizations.

Seeley is widely recognized and admired for her watchdog presence at every City Council meeting and for her incisive interventions at key junctures in Council proceedings to make sure CCSR views are put on the public record. A nurse by profession, her persistence, energy and editorial contributions have made her an important organizer for progressive causes, effective spokesperson for CCSR, and highly-valued campaign worker for progressive City Council candidates.

CBSC (the Coalition for a Better Sonoma County), the third 'horse' of the troika, was established only in 2002 at the initiative of State

Assembly Member Noreen Evans. Its mission statement echoes that of SCCA and CCSR – "to ensure our local government acts for the benefit of all people, not just for the benefit of big money." CBSC brings together environmentalists, labor union members and neighborhood activists, and its website (www.bettersonoma.com) lists 15 participating organizations, chiefly local labor unions, along with a like number of elected officials, comprising Evans, State Senator Pat Wiggins and an array of City Council members from around the County.

CBSC played a pivotal role in the 2008 elections in support of progressives as a vehicle for independent expenditures (IE) – the kind of entity that functions under state law to support (or oppose) candidates separately from candidates' campaign committees. IE money collected and spent by CBSC does not count against campaign spending limits imposed on the candidates themselves. Viewed from the outside, CBSC appears to have fallen short of its founders' expectations. As of early 2010, its last newsletter was dated "Winter 2006," and its website after a period of neglect was back under construction.

In the 2008 election cycle, CBSC also undertook two public opinion polls and a small number of aggressive mailings at both the county and city levels as independent expenditures (IE). Utilizing the talent of graphic designer Sonia Taylor, the CBSC mailers were eye-catching and doubtless effective at what they set out to do. Progressives could credibly claim that such material was justified as a way to get relevant information out to the voters as a balance against the Press Democrat's pro-developer bias. IE mailers from both sides seemed more prevalent in 2008 than they had been in 2006.

ORGANIZING PROGRESSIVE 'NON-SLATES'

Progressive candidates run as loose coalitions, not slates, but in 2008, progressives came closer to forming an organized slate than they had in previous years. Two of the three central organizations – SCCA and CBSC – plus a close ally, the Housing Advocacy Group, joined in October 2007 to publicly endorse Michael Allen, Gary Wysocky and Marsha Vas Dupre for three of the four open seats in the election to be held November 2008. CCSR might have chimed in, but held to its longstanding practice of interviewing the full range of progressive candidates before choosing whom to endorse, and a year in advance of elections was simply too early for that procedure.

SCCA stressed that there was a new unity of progressives underpinning the unusually early endorsements for the 2008 elections. Its press release stated: "Joining SCCA in endorsing these candidates, in a sign of progressive solidarity, are the Housing Advocacy Group (HAG), and the Coalition for a Better Sonoma County (CBSC). This is perhaps the first time in history that these three organizations have not only endorsed candidates in a race this early, but they also have agreed that the three endorsed candidates are the best for all areas of progressive idealism." The timing gave the three candidates a head start on raising money and building name recognition.

Part of the motivation for early endorsements was doubtless also to discourage an excess of candidates. In the past, progressives more than once had in effect shot themselves in the foot by crowding the field with more candidates than open seats, thus taking votes one from the other to the benefit of the more disciplined growth machine, which avoided similar problems by selecting and backing only as many candidates as there were spaces on the ballot. The SCCA-HAG-CSBC initiative did help progressives rally around four candidates for the four regular openings, although they ended up with two competing candidates for the single special election slot on the ballot to complete the term left unfinished by the untimely demise of Mayor Bob Blanchard.

When CCSR did get around to endorsing candidates in early 2008, it gave the nod to the same three as its sister organizations: Allen, Dupre and Wysocky, but it also endorsed Lee Pierce for the fourth open seat. Pierce did not get an endorsement from SCCA because he declined to make an explicit commitment to support SCCA principles – as Pierce told others, it was not that he necessarily disagreed with the substance, but it was important to him to preserve both the fact and appearance of independence to the fullest. CBSC, however, did include Pierce with the other three in its IE campaign mailers, supporting him as one of four progressive "super-heroes" in the election home stretch.

In the race for the single two-year seat to complete Blanchard's term, two progressive candidates threw their hats in the ring. First was David Rosas, who had originally declared for the four-year seat, but had been unable to garner endorsements from the progressive political troika partly because there were doubts he could mount a strong enough campaign to win on his first time out. The four other leading progressive candidates (including Pierce) were given much better chances than Rosas, and in any event, on the advice of friends and progressive supporters Rosas shifted to the two-year race, picking up numerous assurances of assistance, since, win or lose, it appeared initially that he would not be competing against other progressives.

Independent of Rosas, however, neighborhood activist Judy Kennedy saw the unexpected vacancy for the two-year seat as an opportunity for her. She therefore registered as a candidate for that spot on the ballot at virtually the same time as Rosas. While she had numerous supporters among neighborhood and environmental advocates, some had already made commitments to Rosas and were unwilling to renege. As things turned out, both Kennedy and Rosas stayed on the ballot, both gained the endorsement of CCSR, Rosas alone was backed by SCCA, Kennedy alone by the Democratic Central Committee, and neither Kennedy nor Rosas was officially supported by CBSC.

WHO'S IN CHARGE HERE?

Whether one sees it as a strength or weakness, the progressive side in Santa Rosa politics has no Karl Rove to direct its political campaigns. It does have two professionals, Guy Conner and Terry Price, who work actively to help the progressive cause. Their ability to coordinate events at election time, however, is not even close to the quarterback role for the growth machine played by Herb Williams, who managed the campaigns of all five slate candidates in the City Council elections of 2008. That compares to Price, who managed the campaigns of two progressive candidates (Allen and Kennedy), and Conner, who did not manage any.

Nonetheless, the duo of Conner and Price with their expertise have given progressive campaigners an appreciation of political realities, insights into professional campaigning requirements, and a collective sense of direction. Conner as noted above is a board member of all three of the progressives' lead political organizations and Price is on two. They can advise on activities between elections, help progressive groups plan longer-range strategy and assist with campaigns, but conforming to legal requirements, they do not participate in IE activities related to any given candidate if they have any role in that particular candidate's campaign.

Noreen Evans and Pat Wiggins have also been critically important to progressive cohesion and vigor. By virtue of their positions in the State Legislature and prior experience as City Council Members, the two have been the senior progressive political figures in the community. Their endorsements and fund raising assistance has given weight to any progressive's political campaign. Evans in particular has also been a critical driving force for progressive organization, having among other initiatives while still a City Council Member convened the meeting in March 2002 that preceded formation of CBSC, with its platform of principles and procedure to support candidates for the Council and SR Junior College Board. In 2008, she also contributed to funding of CBSC Independent Expenditures.

In addition to the four sitting Council members and two State legislators, in 2010 the wider circle of influential progressives is studded with a range of community leaders. Many are noted above on the Boards of SCCA, CCSR and CBSC. Especially prominent also on the political side are former Council Member Steve Rabinowitsh and Michael Allen, Director of Senator Wiggins Santa Rosa Office as

SR'S PROGRESSIVE DOYENNES PAT WIGGINS AND NOREEN EVANS

The anomaly of Santa Rosa city politics is illustrated by the successful political careers of these two exceptional progressive leaders from Santa Rosa. Local voters send progressives from the City Council to Sacramento by wide margins, but growth machine Mayors and Council Members don't stand a chance for state office.

Both Pat Wiggins and Noreen Evans won election to the City Council in the mid-1990s and worked hard for progressive causes, but were regularly frustrated by the growth machine majorities that dominated Council business. Both went on to the State legislature where they achieved outstanding results.

Wiggins, who served six years in the Assembly and a four-year term in the Senate, founded the Smart Growth Caucus and authored numerous important bills on land use, agriculture, environmental protection and housing, among others. Illness prevented her from running for a second term in 2010.

Evans also compiled an admirable Assembly record working for families and children, environmental protection, legal system reform and promotion of California wine. When Wiggins announced retirement in 2010, Evans campaigned as odds-on favorite to replace her in the Senate.

well as a former SEIU executive. Also worthy of special mention are Rick Theis, founder of the Leadership Institute for Ecology and the Economy and David Grabill of the Housing Advocacy Group.

Coordination of progressive efforts to work on issues (as opposed to elections) improved markedly with the establishment in 2005 of the Accountable Development Coalition (ADC). Its roots hark back to 2002, when Noreen Evans gathered progressives to form CBSC and in parallel a small group of primarily labor advocates set up an entity called New Economy Working Solutions (NEWS). As its name suggests, NEWS focused on economic issues, with an educational orientation and a mission to raise living standards and promote economic equity (website at www.neweconomynorthbay.org). NEWS and CBSC leaders played major roles to set up ADC and give the progressive movement a more substantial lobbying capability. ADC has not endorsed City Council candidates.

ADC has proven an effective focal point for public education on "hot button" progressive issues on the agendas of the City Council or Planning Commission. It bills itself as "a grassroots organization made up of unions, affordable housing advocates, environmentalists, transit and land use experts, and other community-based groups" and describes its mission as promoting "smart growth principles in order to create livable, environmentally sustainable communities with shared prosperity." ADC has a paid Executive Director, currently (2010) Marlene Dehlinger, and maintains a website at www.accountabledevelopmentcoalition.org. ADC's first Executive Director, Jessica Diaz, played a leading role on the City's Green Building Advisory Committee, before being hired away to become Staff Assistant to Supervisor Shirlee Zane.

WHERE'S THE MONEY?

Progressives anywhere typically seek the bulk of their financial support from the grassroots – a few dollars each from a large number of individuals. This is true in Santa Rosa for City Council candidates who still depend primarily on fundraisers at the neighborhood level, donations in small amounts from friends and supporters, and in many cases their personal savings. As confirmed by the experience of David Rosas and the remarks of Mike Martini quoted above in this chapter, growth machine supporters tend to write checks, while progressive grass roots organizations look more to give non-monetary support.

The 2008 campaign was, however, something of a reversal from the patterns of previous years. Contributions from labor unions to progressives were higher than before, in large measure to support Michael Allen, who amassed the biggest campaign war chest. Other progressives continued to finance their campaign with donations from the grassroots, as exemplified, for example, by Marsha Vas Dupre, who ranked second in total spending, but drew her funding support from a very broad list marked by relatively small donations.

Looking ahead, individual progressives will still have to rely primarily on small contributions from individuals and canvassing support from organizations like SCCA. From there, progressives can hope the successful coalition building of the last few years will give labor unions reason to continue their financial participation, even if they do not have a candidate in the race who could be considered "one of their own."

THE HARD PART

In local politics, progressives often lack staying power. Their base tends to be fragmented and oriented toward specific issues, for example, a green building ordinance, a neighborhood park, or a senior center. Absent an immediate cause, it can be hard to mobilize the troops. This pluralism and issue-orientation also makes it difficult to sustain central coordination once the excitement of an election victory gets muted by the mundane press of municipal business – or, as was the case in the wake of the path-breaking 2008 win, the emotional drain of unavoidable budget deficits in a free-fall economy.

Can the progressives on the City Council keep up the political momentum? They brought a new style and sense of priorities to City Hall following the elections of 2008 with more attention to openness and citizen engagement in government, environmental protection, diversity and affordable housing, walkable/bikable downtown development, and dealing with traffic congestion. That is a good start, but many would say the Council majority needs to work harder to put a progressive stamp on city policy if it is to retain strong voter support in 2010 and beyond.

Success in upcoming election campaigns will also necessitate sustained enthusiasm at the grassroots level. Progressive non-profits can help keep the ball rolling as their specific issues come to the fore or require action at the City level. SCCA and ADC, with their paid staff and broad public education objectives, can play an invaluable role by calling attention to progressive objectives and pulling the community together on action issues. Greenbelt Alliance and the Sierra Club can help immensely by continuing to emphasize the importance of broad policy change to meet the sustainability challenges of the coming decades.

Finally, political realities dictate that the progressives' political troika – CCSR, SCCA and CSBC – work to provide continuity and forward planning. That means strengthened coordinating efforts and year-round strategies to develop potential candidates and counter pro-growth propagandizing. In this regard, there should be no doubt that the growth machine's political arm plans ahead continuously – it has the incentives, financial resources and in-place expertise to begin its campaign planning the day after the last election. And its disciplined approach, along with year-round public opinion polling capabilities give it a significant leg up compared to the much more loosely organized progressive groups.

Still, the progressive coalition's primary advantage is an impressive one – its messages and calls to action on environmental protection and social justice issues have broad appeal in Santa Rosa. Progressive goals are more in tune with the views of the local electorate than the pro-developer machine's promotion of profit-driven growth. The challenge for progressives is to articulate the importance of sustainability and demonstrate that they can deliver on their promises to govern effectively.

The competition for Council seats will continue hot and heavy, with ideological overtones. The next two chapters examine where Santa Rosa finds itself in the wake of the "great recession," and what's at stake as the city moves away from the free-wheeling auto-oriented development of the last fifty years to face up to the challenges of sustainability for the next fifty.

CHAPTER 8

WHERE WE ARE – CROSSROADS, CHALLENGE AND CHANGE

Santa Rosa has a great climate and a terrific location near to the sea, the mountains and the metropolis of San Francisco. Luther Burbank's effusive assertion still resonates with many residents: "I would rather own a piece of land the size of a good healthy house lot in Sonoma County than an entire farm anywhere else on earth." By almost any measurement, the city still ranks high as a desirable place to live, and has a promising economic base.

But what must be done to best sustain residents' well-being? Global warming, economic recession, water issues and demographic changes all suggest that our fair city has come to a crossroads. Many Santa Rosans worried that times were changing even before the nation's economic crisis struck full-blown in 2008, and by 2010 with recovery slowly underway, they sensed there would not be a return to business as usual.

Retrofitting physical Santa Rosa for the 21st century seems essential, but it will be no easy job. The pro-growth policies of the past have left the city chopped in half by a highway that can't be moved, hobbled by a strip mall traffic nightmare, frustrated by a hodgepodge downtown and stuck with auto-dependent suburbs. And our city budget is running short of revenues to pay the bills.

The city's legacy from the last few decades also includes the pro-developer electoral machine, along with ongoing pressures for development of open space, especially in the southern reaches of the

City and on the hillsides to the southeast. The local political tussle is now over how to manage future growth and where to put it. This chapter examines the challenges Santa Rosans must confront to articulate a realistic and sustainable vision for their city's future.

AT A CROSSROADS

Santa Rosans have deep appreciation for their city and like living here. Indeed, a nation-wide study conducted in 2009 found that "people in Sonoma County are happier and healthier than anywhere else in California – and ranked fifth overall in the nation." The poll by Gallup-Healthways ranked Sonoma County fifth nationally "in healthy behavior and 16th in work experience, which measures job satisfaction. (The County) ranked 32nd in physical health and 33rd in emotional health."[41]

But the city's residents are still unsure about what comes next. Such doubt is hardly surprising given the environmental pressures and economic worries that have been thrust upon Santa Rosa over the last few years. Looking ahead, there is a broad recognition that we are not in the usual business cycle with a downturn that will simply run its course and then let us end up back more or less where we were.

Root causes of current problems lie far beyond our city limits. New York Times columnist Thomas Friedman in early 2009 concluded, "the whole growth model we created over the last 50 years is simply unsustainable economically and ecologically and that 2008 was when we hit the wall – when Mother Nature and the market both said: "No more."[42] Friedman's fifty-year time frame corresponds essentially to America's post-WW II auto-dependent growth spurt, which carried a willing and eager Santa Rosa along with it.

How to best prepare for the changed times ahead? In 2006, with funding mostly from the City, the Chamber of Commerce undertook an updating of the old city slogan – "city designed for living" – and hired a Tennessee firm that started off with a survey to find out what local notables thought about their city. Reporting on the response, a Press Democrat article observed, "The one vision that stood out from the sampling of those who responded to the survey of (community) leaders is that Santa Rosa is literally at a crossroads."[43] There was no obvious consensus on which way to turn. (Nor was the new slogan, "California Cornucopia," greeted with any noticeable enthusiasm.)

Santa Rosa's overall prosperity is not under any immediate threat. The later more complete version of the Chamber's survey recorded a generally positive, upbeat citizen assessment – "Santa Rosans see their city as the cultural, financial and service hub of Sonoma County, a place that offers much for families and balances urban and rural life styles."[44] Still, the report carried forward doubts about where to go from here, noting that "Santa Rosa is seen as a city that is in transition as it struggles with its own growth."

LEGACY OF GROWTH – CITY DESIGNED FOR CARS[45]

No one really worried about greenhouse gases through the post-WW II decades. During those years, Santa Rosa successfully chased the American dream of prosperity – single-family houses in the suburbs, shopping malls, cars, movie theaters, and more cars. As America's economy expanded, so did our fair city, and the process worked well for the majority of Santa Rosa's residents, although not for everyone and not without unintended consequences.

Our city leaders seized the opportunity to advance concrete proposals for growth and development when World War II came to an end. Citizens endorsed their plans, and financing was secured with a 1-cent sales tax and an increased business license tax. In tandem with municipal improvements, Junior College classes swelled with students under the GI bill, businesses prospered, homes were built, Sears Roebuck arrived as did a baseball team, and Memorial Hospital rose on the edge of downtown. A contest for a slogan to capture the times was won by a local high school girl, Marilyn Johnson, with the phrase mentioned above: "A City Designed for Living."

The post-War generation of Santa Rosa movers and shakers built for the auto. Politics followed economics as developers, bankers, mortgage companies and real estate interests – the elements of the classic "growth machine" described in Chapter 4 – took over the reins of power to exploit America's growing mobility with its thirst for suburbs and shopping malls. "Political power was shifting, not so subtly, away from the agricultural forces and the merchants, spelling the end of Santa Rosa as a farm town," observed Gaye LeBaron, Santa Rosa's resident historian extraordinaire, and co-author Joann Mitchell in *Santa Rosa: A Twentieth Century Town.*[46]

Legendary developer Hugh Codding, bankers like Charles Renking and Henry Keegan, mortgage brokers led by Henry Trione, and suppliers like Elie Destruel of Meade Clark Lumber Company formed the early growth machine that shaped the city. They may have disagreed amongst themselves – firebrand Codding had a clear penchant for going his own way – but at the end of the day, what was good for them collectively was good for Santa Rosa. Highway 101 was kept in place and expanded, suburbs sprawled outward, and shopping malls sprang up at key locations.

The combination of autos, roads and available large land tracts around Santa Rosa beckoned with high profit potential. Developers were eager to help home-buyers obtain dream houses with lawns and garages. The flamboyant and entrepreneurial Codding transformed large swaths of land and single-handedly produced a town and shopping center of his own – Montgomery Village opened in 1950. But Codding could not muster the resources for water and other city services, so he consented to annexation in 1955, and Santa Rosa nearly doubled in population overnight to over 31,000 residents. The city took "its place among the growth-oriented medium-sized urban centers of the San Francisco Bay area."[47] Problems created by

CHRISTINE CULVER BICYCLE ADVOCATE – ENGAGED CITIZEN

When Christine Culver moved to Santa Rosa in 1988 she was an avid bicyclist, with no idea of what local politics were all about. An encounter on her bike in 2001 with an uninformed Mercedes driver inspired her to make a life U-turn to work on public education and bicycle rights. Google took her to the then three month old Sonoma County Bicycle Coalition – she volunteered, went on to part-time work and then became full-time Executive Director.

Culver and the SCBC are great demonstrations that engaged citizens can make a difference – for the public's safety, health, the environment, economic activity, and fun. The Coalition's strong programs for both transportation and recreation work effectively to advance quality of life and sustainability goals.

In Santa Rosa that all requires changing attitudes and retrofitting a city built for the auto. Culver and her SCBC colleagues are helping to catalyze critical changes in planning, making streets safer for all users, and spreading the word on bicycle benefits – in short, they have put cycling on the local map.

the auto-centered philosophy of development would only become apparent much later.

THAT BLANKETY-BLANK HIGHWAY

The single most fateful decision affecting Santa Rosa's post-war development was to keep Highway 101 running smack through the center of town. State engineers strongly recommended it be moved to by-pass the city on the west side and most residents agreed, but downtown merchants swung their considerable weight behind successful demands that the freeway continue to carry its traffic close to the town center line.

The upgraded highway was opened in 1949, "the year," a Press Democrat reporter noted, "they sawed the town in half." Whatever the benefits to merchants downtown, the highway as it grew wider and taller invited congestion and compromised aesthetics. The result inspired town wits in 2007 to propose sardonic new town mottos for Santa Rosa: "Bottleneck of the Wine Country," "A Freeway Runs through It," and "Where the Gridlock Meets the Vineyards."

The later construction of Highway 12 then crossed with Highway 101 to split the town into quarters. It would have chopped its way right on through the eastern suburbs and over Spring Lake were it not for one of the most remarkable early efforts to defend the environment within city limits. June Moes marshaled fellow citizens to make sure Highway 12 would not be built to despoil the lake and the relatively new parks then being developed on the east side of the city. The City had put the highway extension in its General Plan, but along with Caltrans shelved the project in the face of an unyielding citizenry. The strip of land, which is ideally suited for greenway or park use, has lain fallow ever since, despite repeated efforts of neighbors in the Bennett Valley area to elicit government approvals for beneficial public use of the property as a greenway.

Today, the two intersecting highways, rising up like dams, disrupt connectivity and create dead spaces. The cost of removing them is now prohibitive, and the city makes do with unattractive underpasses, which discourage bicycle and pedestrian traffic going from one side to the other. This is particularly true of the widest and central-most Highway 101 underpass at Third St., although less of a problem between

Railroad Square and the Plaza Mall garage since there are two flat and relatively open passageways close together with a third scheduled to be added in the near future at 6th St. Planning is underway for a bicycle and pedestrian overpass in the Junior College area where crossing opportunities are more limited.

The problem of connectivity across Highway 101 is becoming more acute as the day approaches when the SMART train will begin operation, projected for 2014. The two Santa Rosa SMART stations will lie just to the west of Highway 101 – the existing historic station at Railroad Square and a new one to be built at Jennings Ave. or near to it. Much of the prospective traffic to and from these two stations will necessarily have to cross the highway to reach key destinations, notably Courthouse Square, the Junior College, the Plaza Mall and Coddingtown Mall, all of which are located on the east side.

AND THOSE BLANKETY-BLANK MALLS

Along with highways and residential suburbs, shopping malls also blossomed in the decades of rapid growth. Most of the smaller ones in Santa Rosa fit in reasonably well with their surroundings, but the downtown Plaza Mall and the string of strip malls on Santa Rosa Avenue present major problems for the city's future development. The Santa Rosa Avenue stores regularly generate traffic gridlock, and the Plaza Mall's massive presence compounds the city's division.

At the time they were built, both malls were hailed by the reigning growth machine politicians as forward-looking projects that would revitalize the city after a period of decline followed by a destructive earthquake. "During the 1960s, the downtown area of Santa Rosa was badly deteriorating. A new redevelopment agency was formed to reverse the trend, but progress was initially slow. Streets and buildings were sub-standard, many buildings remained vacant and boarded up, and lower-income senior citizens occupied older, unsafe, single-room occupancy hotels."[48]

Then came the earthquake of 1969. No one was killed, but the tremors did considerable physical damage when they struck on October 1, the first at 9:56 pm and a second shortly thereafter at 11:19 pm. They were rated moderate at 5.6 and 5.7 respectively on the Richter scale, but they were strong enough that "a number of old brick and wood frame structures were damaged beyond repair. Chimneys toppled, underground pipes ruptured and many walls cracked or collapsed. Virtually every store in downtown Santa Rosa sustained broken windows."[49]

City leaders opted for wholesale make-over of the downtown area. The Santa Rosa Redevelopment project, which had been in place since 1961, helped developers advance ambitious schemes for Third Street as well as for clearing away old buildings on the west side of downtown along the freeway. A new City Manager, Kenneth Blackman, took office in 1970, and proved an enthusiastic supporter of intensified growth policies.

The centerpiece of the new downtown was to be the Santa Rosa Plaza Mall, covering roughly five city blocks. The structure was state of the art for its time – all enclosed and with plenty of parking in a three-story garage. It was a popular concept, although Hugh Codding's all-out resistance and lawsuit delayed its construction. Codding sought to ward off the competition for market share of his nearby Coddingtown Shopping Center, but he lost and the Mall proceeded.

Once built, the Plaza Mall further walled off the Courthouse and Railroad Square districts from each other. City Administration at the time had little foresight or interest in promoting pedestrian and bicycle traffic, so it failed to insist on easement rights for a Plaza Mall cut-through to facilitate movement between the two parts of downtown. Moreover, the garage siting and design encouraged customers to enter from Highway 101, shop, and leave by Highway 101, such that relatively little spill-over benefit materialized for other shopping locales around Railroad or Courthouse Squares.

The city's other problem malls, the shopping centers along Santa Rosa Avenue, were promoted in particular to generate sales tax income after Proposition 13 passed in 1978. The city wooed the first big mall along Santa Rosa Avenue, the Santa Rosa Marketplace now anchored on Costco and Target, with a $3 million sweetener for infrastructure. The initial success attracted other stores along the avenue, bringing choices to consumers and sales tax revenues to the city, but eventually exacerbating traffic problems to the point of recurrent gridlock at peak hours.

The upshot of our two highways and two problem mall complexes has left Santa Rosa with difficult design and development problems to "retrofit" its central districts. Near the center of town, the additional under-crossing at 6th St. and the prospective overpass near the Junior College will help, but not by much. To the South, the fundamental difficulty is overloaded streets, such that a 2008 Environmental Impact Report for a proposed new big box store near the Santa Rosa Ave. malls could only conclude there was no way to avoid making the existing traffic problems worse.[50]

THE ROSELAND DONUT HOLE

One other legacy continuing to bedevil the City is the scattering of county-administered areas left within the city limits. The largest is the remaining piece of Roseland, comprising a 900 acre enclave with about 7,000 people, mostly Latino, who ended up out in the cold, in part because in the past some residents preferred the rural orientation and lower taxes of Sonoma County governance. But the bigger historical factors creating the problem have been economic and developer interests, which led the city to annex profitable investment chunks like the row of car dealerships, but shy away from areas like the last donut hole, which would require substantial investment to bring infrastructure and services up to city standards.

The result is a small Roseland bastion of hodgepodge public services and what amounts to second class citizenship for its residents. Although there is a unified fire district and efforts have been made to coordinate police calls, residents still live with confusion and delays, since the responsibility for law enforcement can depend on whether a criminal suspect is standing on the sidewalk or in the street – the dividing line between city and county often runs along the street edge of the sidewalk, if there is one. More generally, Roseland residents for almost all practical purposes are treated as if they lived in Santa Rosa, except they are not eligible for provision of city services.

Many progressives view annexation as a priority for reasons of social equity. As long as Roseland is a donut hole, divisions are accentuated by the de facto segregation it represents, and made worse by negative perceptions in the minds of well-to-do Santa Rosans, who have little idea of what the area is all about. The City and County intensified negotiations in the mid-2007s, ostensibly making it an issue of not "whether but when." At the time, Mayor Blanchard espoused the objective, but with the proviso that annexation be "revenue neutral" – in real life, that seemed to mean Roseland would never come into the City because there was little prospect of finding the necessary money. In 2009, newly-elected Supervisor Shirlee Zane sought to break the negotiating impasse over estimated costs and move to a more practical approach, which would allow annexation with a phasing in of improvements as resources became available. The City and County approved hiring of a consultant to help with the process.

A related issue, illustrating problems of both legacy and current attitudes, is potential gentrification. The City started in the early 2000s to plan for development of the area, assuming eventual annexation and based on traditional redevelopment models driven by economic feasibility and market demand. With minimum provisions for affordable housing, the probable outcome would be gentrification and displacement over time of most current residents. Magdalena Ridley, a Roseland native and its articulate muse, argued for more equitable alternatives to preserve its thriving multicultural working-class character – she urged that the City not use redevelopment as "just another way in which the lower half is told they don't matter – especially here in Roseland, because we've already heard it enough."[51]

CONSERVING OPEN SPACE AND WATER

Citizen activism to protect Sonoma County's natural beauty outside the city limits took firm root shortly after WW II, but did not reach Santa Rosa town until much later. The city's residential development followed patterns made possible by an intensified urban street network and a car in every garage. In the fashion of the times, housing tracts spread out across neighboring fields and hills, public transit systems got low priority at best, and there was little or no incentive to build higher density housing downtown or even close to potential transit routes.

In the 1980s, however, a general environmental concern to combat urban sprawl emerged in Santa Rosa. Grassroots pressure built state-wide to preserve green space, and Santa Rosa's first General Plan was written in 1991 to establish a more controlled approach to growth and concomitant sprawl. City Manger Blackman and pro-growth advocates controlling the City Council made sure the new Plan was written to accommodate future suburban development on a major scale, resisting environmentalist proposals for more restrictive limits on sprawl. Although the Plan contained commendable provisions for parks and historic preservation, in general it carried forward an unabashed philosophy of continuous growth.

The developer establishment similarly co-opted and limited the impact of Santa Rosa's Urban Growth Boundaries (UGB), which complemented the General Plan and growth management initiatives. A citizen's commission drew up a detailed UGB proposal, but developers and their City Council allies maneuvered to reduce its scope. Bob Higham, Chair of the commission, later told the Press Democrat that then-Mayor Sharon Wright acted as "more of an obstructionist and staller than anything else."[52] Giving way in 1996 when overwhelming public support

> ### CAROLINE BANUELOS
> ### SOCIAL ADVOCATE –
> ### COMMUNITY REPRESENTATIVE
>
> Caroline Banuelos exemplifies the community advocate and volunteer – engaged in organizations involving youth, homelessness, and mental health, as well as being a Santa Rosa Planning Commissioner. She is now (2010) employed with The Living Room, a drop-in center for homeless women and children, and in the past, has worked with the Community Support Network and Social Advocates for Youth, among others. She has also been a paralegal.
>
> What stands out from her community service, however, is dedication and participation within city-wide progressive efforts to help Santa Rosa's Latinos exercise their political voices. Banuelos is President of the Sonoma County Latino Democratic Club, a participant in the Coalition for a Better Sonoma County, and a founder of the Coalition for Latino Civic Engagement. In 2006, she made a good showing in City Council elections, but failed to gain a seat.

became apparent, Wright and her Council colleagues put a rather watered-down measure on the ballot, which passed, but was criticized by many as well short of the mark. In 2010, many environmentalists would still like to see the UGB made smaller, but political realities and procedural impediments make significant change unlikely one way or the other.

Also, the city's growth has come to a point that threatens to outpace its ability to guarantee future delivery of clean water and efficient disposal of waste liquids. Santa Rosa and Sonoma County have been blessed with substantial water supply, although not necessarily in the right place at the right time. The city's official assessment – a Utilities

Department report dated November 25, 2008 and titled SB 610 Water Supply Assessment for Santa Rosa General Plan 2035 – concluded there will be adequate water to cover development through 2035 using a combination of entitlement from the county water authority (SCWA), local groundwater, recycled water and stringent conservation measures. The report was duly approved by the City Council.

But all four projected sources are fraught with uncertainty. On the first count, SCWA, partly in response to new federal requirements for fish protection, in 2009 markedly reduced its projection of deliverable supplies to the city. As for the other three, extraction of local groundwater is essentially unregulated; the cost of recycled water is potentially very high; and the willingness of customers to accept increasingly severe conservation and/or bear higher rates is problematic. Critics also call attention to more realistic, and considerably lower, projections of rainfall that take global warming into account. Water issues and the nagging uncertainties that surround them are discussed in more detail in Chapter10.

The city's legacy includes several other significant environmental and health issues that remain to be dealt with. Some Santa Rosa schools are located in areas with high traffic density, a factor that researchers have identified as a potentially serious cause of asthma and other respiratory problems in children. Also, brownfields have yet to be cleaned up at some sites (the term applies to land plots that cannot be easily reused because of the presence of a hazardous substance, pollutant, or contaminant). Finally, the need to protect tiger salamander habitat and wetland pockets are matters that also must be addressed – a comprehensive plan for the Santa Rosa plain was under discussion, but the whole issue has to be reconsidered after the Obama Administration overturned a laxer approach instituted under its predecessor.

DEMOGRAPHICS – OLDER, LESS ANGLO

Many Santa Rosans seem uneasy about the prospect of population growth and demographic change. According to the County Administration, the county "has continued a modest growth rate, reaching 484,470 residents by 2008. Since 2000, the population had increased by 23,006 residents, or 5.0% ...The City of Santa Rosa has led this growth in total population gain, adding 12,386 residents, or 8.4%, to attain its current (2008) population of 159,981."[53] For perspective, that increase in Santa Rosa alone was equivalent to adding another town larger than either Healdsburg (pop. 2007 est. 11,700) or Sonoma (pop. 2006 est. 9,900).

Official projections show Santa Rosa's population growing to 233,500 people by 2035. Although the rate of increase may seem small – 1 to 2% annually – the result by 2035 will be to add over 70,000 more people to the 2010 population of about 160,000. For comparison, that's roughly equivalent to adding the number of people resident today in Rohnert Park plus Windsor.

There will not only be more people, but their composition will also change dramatically. One trend underway is aging of the city's population – in a 2007 report SSU's Dr. Robert Eyler noted: "The California Department of Finance (DOF) tracks age profile data and makes projections for all of California's counties. For Marin, Napa and Sonoma Counties, the North Bay's core area, data suggest these counties will age significantly over the next fifteen years."[54] "Aging significantly" in this case refers to the projection that the percentage of the population over 50 will grow from about 28% in 2000 to just over 35% in 2025. This percentage will peak in 2021, and then begin to slowly go down as the Latino population increases with a younger average age.

Dr. Eyler also reported, "The DOF ethnicity data suggest that by 2023, the North Bay will be predominantly Latino, if we include Solano County in our calculations. Napa County, by 2032, will be predominantly Latino, while Marin and Sonoma Counties will not be before 2050. Latinos are projected to be the youngest ethnicity in the North Bay through 2050; in Sonoma County, 70% of the Latino population will be under 40 in the year 2015."

These basic trends will probably continue almost no matter what the city does. To benefit from the changes, Santa Rosa will have to stay ahead of the curve with sound education and housing policies. Dr. Eyler concluded the North Bay "must educate its residents to participate in a wide breadth of businesses...prepare its transportation and health care systems for demographic changes; and...decide between housing its residents and its workers, or just housing its residents and importing its workers." His remarks elicited a lot of head-nodding, but no concrete official reactions as of early 2010. Later chapters will address these issues in more detail.

THE LEGACY – POLITICAL AND PHYSICAL

The political legacy of recent decades is in the first instance the experienced, cohesive and smoothly-oiled growth machine described in Chapter 5. Over its years of unbroken City Council control, the pro-developer bloc also enjoyed close relations with City officials and exercised strong influence on the planning process. The result has built in considerable momentum for further large-scale development, perhaps most notably by setting in motion the extension of Farmers Lane to open up the southeast and by paving the way for the annexation of a large tract along Santa Rosa Avenue north of Todd Road.

It is not that developers have had a blank check. The dogged interventions of anti-sprawl environmentalists and social justice advocates put important limits on growth with the Urban Growth Boundary, the Growth Management Ordinance, and the Housing Allocation Plan. Progressive coalitions also had limited success with efforts to promote diversity, inclusivity and citizen engagement in government in the early 2000s.

And difficult choices lie ahead to assure adequate revenues for funding city services. Having focused for the last three decades on developing as a retail center, Santa Rosa is now heavily dependent on sales tax revenue for its discretionary city budget. Its rapid growth has also magnified the importance of continued income from development fees to meet demands for utilities and services. This formula served well for years, but no longer appears adequate for future needs.

On the physical side, as indicated above, the legacy of Santa Rosa's past development poses a variety of challenges for efforts to design a sustainable 21st century city. Residential neighborhoods must be "retrofitted" to reduce energy consumption and provide livability with less reliance on the auto. To sustain downtown's vitality will take imagination and investment to develop its limited spaces and overcome the connectivity issues posed by the highway and Plaza Mall. Nor will it be easy or cheap to implement new transit-oriented development strategies and take maximum advantage of the SMART train service.

Unbridled growth was Santa Rosa's mantra through the end of the 20th century. Sustainability has become the test of the 21st century, and the transition is proving difficult. The next chapter looks at the state of city planning – how it works, where state and federal requirements fit in, what needs to be changed, and the ongoing political contest to control the process.

CHAPTER 9

PLANNING AHEAD – HOW AND FOR WHAT?

Charting future development for a good-sized city like Santa Rosa is no simple task when circumstances change as much as they have in recent years. New initiatives are needed, but that means redirecting the considerable momentum built into existing plans, zoning codes, infrastructure investments and the like. To stop or significantly modify many of these activities in mid-stream would put at risk millions of public and private dollars.

The planning challenges that face Santa Rosa for the next quarter century are complex: a population projected to grow from near 160,000 in 2010 to over 233,000 in 2035; higher percentages of Latinos and the elderly; an uncertain economic recovery for the next few years; unrelenting pressures on the city budget; and arched over all, the critical need to correctly define and then achieve "sustainability." To make progress, the city will have to accommodate the realities of infrastructure shortcomings and resolve local disagreement over how best to proceed, partly masked by General Plan sections that present differing visions of the future.

The political shift of recent years has begun to significantly redirect the city's planning. The Station Area Specific Plan (SASP), approved in 2007, marked an important milestone on the way to transit-oriented development and more inclusive housing policies. Subsequent city planning efforts have hewed to the SASP model with greater attention to environmental sustainability, social justice, Smart Growth and "complete neighborhoods." Although supportive in principle of more "green" business, the developer community and its political arm have mounted vigorous efforts to keep the pendulum from swinging away from the models of the past.

The following sections examine the visions that are guiding Santa Rosa's planning for development, the realities that set limits to what can be done, the plans now on the table, and the on-going tensions generated by differing views on how those plans should be implemented.

START WITH A VISION

Urban visioning – expressing residents' idea of what their city should look like in the future – is a deceptively simple exercise. In most cases, when citizens from all walks of life get together, they soon find much immediate common ground on goals like safe streets, thriving neighborhoods, healthy economic activity, good roads with free flowing traffic, and clean water from home faucets. Moreover, in Santa Rosa there has also been general recognition that urban sprawl should be held in check, and hence in the early 1990s citizens voted for growth management measures and an Urban Growth Boundary, the latter now in force through 2016. More recently, there seems a broad acceptance of the need for "sustainability" in the 21st century. Forging consensus on how to achieve a broad and ideal vision, however, becomes more difficult at each succeeding level of specificity – stymied by the proverbial devil in the details.

And that is where planning comes in. It is the mechanism to bridge from idealized visions to completed projects on the ground. The American Planning Association describes the task this way: "Planning helps community members …find the right balance of new development and essential services, protection of the environment, and innovative change." It is popular these days also to add some reference to *sustainability*, meaning to plan so that future generations will in no way be deprived of benefits and opportunities equal or greater to those we plan for ourselves.

Santa Rosa has in hand an official vision of what Santa Rosa should be like in 2035 – the end of the period described in the City's General Plan 2035. The vision sections of the document by and large set forth the kind of cultured generalities and desirable objectives noted above:

vibrant community…maintain the local quality of life…safe livable residential neighborhoods…downtown as the heart of the community… many streets with a boulevard character …public art…and so forth. Similarly ideal formulations have characterized General Plans since the first was produced in 1991.

That is not to say that the vision-drawing process is static. The newest version of the Plan, approved in late 2009, significantly adds an emphasis on making Santa Rosa "a regional leader in environmental stewardship." Responding to the intensified public desire to tackle global warming, the Plan is careful to incorporate references to the ambitious GHG reduction goals adopted by City Councils. And in the same vein, wherever appropriate, the text picks up on environmental sustainability themes.

Visioning downtown Santa Rosa is a special case. The area – from the railroad station east to E St. and from College south to Sonoma Ave. – is, as the General Plan states, the "heart" of the city, literally and figuratively. West of the freeway, Railroad Square and West End Districts have by dint largely of their own efforts retained distinctive characters. The Station Area Specific Plan lays out a cogent vision for the area around the station, but east of the freeway it is less notable since no truly cohesive scheme for development has emerged to fill in behind the withered dreams of a high-rise city center. Progress has been made, to be sure, on reunification of Courthouse Square itself, although that will not be accomplished for a long time since it must be done with privately-raised funds, and as of early 2010, estimates had ballooned to around $14 million. Other ideas waiting for leadership to pull them together into a cohesive new vision for downtown include a major performing arts center, a new City Hall complex, and more residential buildings.

In 2006/7, the City Administration launched a visioning survey outside the regular General Plan process. Dubbed *Santa Rosa 2030* and described in an official brochure of that name on the city website, the key elements are more graphic than the General Plan's cautious language. Respondents to a 2030 survey said they wanted the city to keep Santa Rosa's "small town character," create "breath-taking open spaces," and make downtown "more vital." These phrases have an appealing ring to many, and point in a rather different direction from the more intense high-rise development model long dominant in Santa Rosa. But the impact of SR 2030 has been limited, and the City has yet to explain how it can be melded with GP 2035, which rests far more solidly on the state-mandated planning process.

REALITY CHECKS

Ideal city visions – like we have in Santa Rosa – are inevitably cut down to size by real-life constraints. For openers, in card-player jargon, there is the hand we have been dealt – the infrastructure limitations and resource uncertainties discussed in the previous chapter. The malls and Highway 101 are here to stay, much of our water supply has already been committed, and demographics are changing inexorably. Planning has to adapt to these realities.

Plans in the North Bay area of California must also accommodate strong citizen interest in protection of the environment and social justice – two themes which have long been inspirational goals for a legion of area residents. Open space, coastal access, habitat protection, clean water, breathable air, toxic clean-up and countering sprawl are still high on the agenda for Santa Rosa and surrounding municipalities. Affordable housing needs have also surged to the fore in recent years as a top priority for civic activists, and they have backing from state and federal authorities. Accomplishing these environmental and social objectives, however, costs money and necessarily requires curbing some aspects of development. These competing pressures are examined with more detail in the next three chapters of this book.

On the resource side, the budget crunches of 2008/9/10 have demonstrated how increasingly difficult it is to find money for roads, public safety coverage, and parks, which themselves don't produce enough revenue to be self-supporting. In general also, residential development simply does not generate enough money to pay for needed infrastructure and city services. Part of the difference is made up by collecting fees from each new development project, but that still falls short in Santa Rosa and, moreover, drives up the cost of housing. Commercial construction comes closer to paying its way, and Santa Rosa has steadily increased development and impact fees for that sector.

SACRAMENTO AND WASHINGTON

National and State requirements heavily impact any municipality's planning. Provoked by poor local-level performance over many years – more so elsewhere than in Santa Rosa – a number of mandatory measures are now in force to set standards for health, safety and equity. Failure on the part of the City to meet, for example, requirements to provide facilities for the disabled or to observe minimum environmental safety levels can bring lawsuits to assure compliance with legislation. Other standards – such as for housing, education and transportation – are effectively 'enforced' by linkage to availability of federal or state grants, which cities desperately need in California where their taxing authority has been strictly limited since the passage of Proposition 13 in 1978.

In Santa Rosa's case, state and federal grant funding is significant for transportation, housing and environmental protection. Transportation, for example, is a costly affair – one mile of two lane road can cost $3 million or more in rural areas, $5 million or more in urban settings. Developers paid for the Fountaingrove Parkway and recouped their costs through profits on construction and sales of homes in the city's fanciest, most costly residential area, but many criticized the project on aesthetic as well as safety grounds. The pattern is not likely to be repeated, although the City continues to pursue an extension for Farmers Lane, which would open up development in the southeast quadrant. This and any other major road construction will surely require a major infusion of funds from government sources – at a time of increased funding competition and pressures to reduce reliance on road travel.

ABAG MAKES US DO IT!?

ABAG, the Association of Bay Area Governments, presents itself as "leading the region in advocacy, collaboration, and excellence in planning, research, and member services."[55] It makes long term forecasts for population, housing and employment throughout the Bay Area, and sets "Performance Targets" to identify environmental, land-use and transportation related impacts of growth. Although ABAG has taken pains to deny that its targets are mandates, cities like Santa Rosa continue to take them as de facto requirements. Whether the ABAG numbers are mandatory or not, failure to make credible efforts to meet ABAG targets can hurt a city's ability to obtain grant funding, especially to help with affordable housing.

In practice, ABAG's targets have been among the most important factors influencing planning for growth in Santa Rosa. ABAG is the final arbiter of a state-mandated process for determining how many housing units, including a minimum percentage of affordable units, each community must plan to accommodate as its share of regional growth needs. The California Department of Housing and Community Development determines the total housing need for a region, and ABAG takes it from there with an allocation formula based on projected household (i.e., population) growth, existing employment and estimated job growth, and weighting factors to encourage housing near transit.

That kind of dry description drawn from ABAG's website begs a host of questions. It is hard, for example, to understand how it came to be that all of Marin County (population near 250,000) has a target of 4,882 units for 2007-2014, while for the same period, Santa Rosa alone (population about 157,000) is tasked with 6,534 units. Rightly or wrongly for many in Sonoma County, cold statistical explanations seem to mask a basic unfairness or at least politicized decision-making. There is also the much broader chicken and egg question of whether the State/ABAG process is essentially "an advocate for real estate development interests" or "merely gives fair warning of what's surely coming down the pike while simultaneously advancing environmental aims and social goals of population diversity and job growth."[56]

In any case, Santa Rosa and other cities can resist ABAG targets, but cannot completely ignore them without risk of punishment. A number of municipalities have gotten away with far worse compliance records than Santa Rosa, but when Pleasanton voted an overall cap on housing units, it eventually wound up in court, sued by housing advocates joined by the State Attorney General. Santa Rosa itself was taken to court in 2002 by the local Housing Advocacy Group for failing to specify sufficient land for residential development in its General Plan, and soon settled by agreeing to measures that assured increased land availability to meet ABAG targets.

More frequently than lawsuits, stipulations for grants pressure cities to fall in line with state and ABAG priorities. State and federal agencies increasingly give preference to those grant applications that have the higher percentage of low-cost housing in their projects. In June 2009, for example, the developer of Santa Rosa's Railroad Square partnering with the City, won an $11.4 million grant for the SMART area project, in part by sweetening the application (over objections from some nearby residents) with clear commitments to affordable housing. Conversely, the chances of getting the grant would have been lowered if the project had not played up to ABAG priorities.

THE MOTHER PLAN

Santa Rosa's General Plan, mentioned above, is by California law, the definitive guide for development. It must be comprehensive, long-range and internally consistent. It numbers over 350 pages and for most non-specialists, is a complex, even mysterious, force that "guides the city's planning and zoning functions as well as the funding of public improvement projects, such as parks and streets."[57] Although pointed in a general direction, there is a bewildering array of goals, plans, directives, encouragements, and policy guidelines that can seemingly be cherry-picked by planners and lawyers to support whichever project is most fashionable or has the most political oomph of the day.

The heart of the General Plan is its Land Use Diagram, a map of the city planning area showing what can be built where. As required by state law, each classification is marked distinctively, for example with colors and symbols or graphic patterns, to show locations of commercial and residential zones, along with features like schools and parks. The colors are gradated to indicate ranges for population density and building intensity, providing in the process information required to determine traffic circulation, needs for public facilities and adjustments for environmental constraints. Since Santa Rosa is mostly "built out," the city's Land Use Diagram tends to show what is already there – bright red blocks downtown and along main roads correspond to business concentrations, large swatches of pale yellow spread across the map show low density residential tracts, and so on.

The importance of the map – and the power of the City Council that fixes its prosaic patchwork of color – becomes apparent only when one zooms in on parcels that have yet to be developed to their full monetary potential. Bits of vacant or formerly agricultural land may be worth little if reserved for open space or they may be worth a great deal of money if the color shows zoning for commercial use or highly profitable residential construction. Small fortunes still ride on the final coloring of lots now empty in southeast Santa Rosa waiting for Farmers Lane to be extended, space for development on the Imwalle Gardens farm near the railroad station, and prime infill parcels scattered about town. And what's there now can be changed by Council fiat, although any new coloring must still be consistent with state requirements such as those for environmental protections and housing needs.

Of course there's much more in the General Plan than a map. "The General Plan contains hundreds of policies which guide the daily decision making of the City Council and city boards and commissions," according to the 2008 Annual Review.[58] State law mandates that seven topics be covered: land use, circulation, conservation, open space, safety, noise, and housing. Santa Rosa's document is expanded to 13 Chapters, covering not only the specific State requirements, but also the vision discussed above, economic vitality, urban design, historic preservation, and arts and culture.

Santa Rosa's General Plan is a solid document, literally and figuratively. The staff that wrote the Plan is very professional, its policies are sensitive to state and federal requirements, its guidance is detailed, and its thrust is attuned to the times. Despite its strong legal standing as *the* authority for all city planning, however, at the end of the day, the General Plan provides more advice than direction; its provisions are subject to interpretation; and the City Council majority can – when it wishes – simply amend it to serve the interests of political supporters.

Recognizing such limitations, the State Legislature has progressively tightened the politically sensitive housing requirements, and at the local level, civic activists have engineered voter-mandated growth restrictions that cannot be reversed by City Council actions. Though both housing and growth have regular chapters in the General Plan, both also are treated in separate program documents framed by Ordinances first initiated in 1992. Thus, the Housing Allocation Plan (HAP) and Growth Management Ordinance (GMO) follow General Plan directions, but have specific requirements of their own, and annual reports on their implementation must be made to the City Council.

The Growth Management Ordinance is intended to impose limits on the rate of residential growth to assure both adequate infrastructure, including police and fire services, and a reasonable proportion of affordable housing units. It does so by limiting the number of housing permits issued to a base of 900 per year (through 2010), of which one half or 450 units must be of a generally affordable type. To accommodate practical problems such as construction or financing delays, the ordinance allows carry-overs, some trades between categories and "banking" of unused permits for a later time. With housing demand booming in 2006, the pro-developer Council majority freed up 1,000 banked permits for issuance with "no strings attached,"[59] but the demand evaporated as the recession kicked in, and many of the projects went into foreclosure after the housing boom went bust. In 2008, only 176 permits were issued.

The HAP is designed, in the words of the General Plan, "to increase the number of affordable housing units in the community." To this end, it has mandated that on the basis of acreage, large housing projects must include a percentage of affordable units built on site, while smaller projects can pay "in lieu" fees into the City's housing fund, which also draws from Redevelopment Agency monies as well as state and federal grants. Overall, the scheme has met ABAG housing targets for low- and moderate-income residents, but has come up way short for very low income groups and, critics charge, has promoted "ghetto-ization" by concentrating city-subsidized projects on the west and south sides of town.

CHANGING COURSE...FINALLY?

Progressives have been pushing hard for many years to make Santa Rosa's development policies more responsive to environmental protection and social justice goals. City Councils dominated by growth coalition interests made some important concessions such as to allow the Urban Growth Boundary, but only under heavy political pressure. By and large pro-developer Council Members have used their majority powers to control the City's planning agenda and frame language in the General Plan that minimized restrictions on growth and development.

A closer look at the General Plan shows how citizen input was co-opted and then shunted to the back burners of the planning process. In 2000/2001 a group of elected and appointed officials and public members, called the Public Management Team (PMT), was convened to get citizen input for the then-upcoming revision of the General Plan. The PMT met regularly to discuss planning issues and hosted 12 widely advertised community meetings, three in each quadrant of the city, to get community input. From its extensive work, the PMT drafted a set of "Guiding Principles," building in ideas then coming to the fore about alternative transportation, higher density transit-oriented housing, diversity and strengthened environmental protection. These Guiding Principles provided strongly progressive elements of a roadmap for Santa Rosa's future course.

The PMT statement has been recorded in the General Plan, starting with its overview introduction:

> *Santa Rosa is a special place set in an agricultural county with an inviting climate, superior natural beauty, desirable residential neighborhoods, and a strong, diversified economy. As the area accepts its share of the region's growth, these characteristics must not be sacrificed. Instead, the growth must protect the positive qualities which make the city attractive and build new features which provide enduring value and beauty and further improve the quality of life. It is our duty to assure that, twenty years from now, Santa Rosa is an even more desirable city than it is today.*

Twenty-one short Principles are then listed after the above statement. For progressives at least, the approach has remained valid, even inspiring, and nearly a decade after they were written, the Principles stand up well to more recently articulated demands of the 21st century. Their potentially far-reaching guidelines include:

-- no new development without provision for adequate infrastructure;
-- pedestrians=cars=bikes on all streets in Santa Rosa;
-- conserve and showcase natural assets such as creeks, trees and skylines;
-- improve connectivity across town;
-- address the entire spectrum of housing needs;

-- commit to sustainable development practices;
-- focus employment strategies on existing businesses;
-- expand art and culture.

The City Council back in 2000 to 2004 did not, however, buy into the PMT statement. The language was reproduced in the General Plan, but as little more than decoration. The Council directed that "The Guiding Principles are advisory only and do not represent General Plan policy." So much for over a year's work by a broad-based commission with extensive public out-reach. When the General Plan came up for review in 2008/9, the progressive majority chose not to reenergize the PMT, deciding to focus specifically on the Housing Element largely because of budget distractions and Mayor Gorin's hopes to overcome partisanship.

But the ideas of the PMT General Principles remained alive, and in the last few years, Santa Rosa's planning has inched in their direction. Parallel with the political shifts from 2004 to 2008, increased grassroots activism has helped bring about greater attention to the concerns of advocates for environmental protection, social justice and more livable neighborhoods. The concrete embodiment of the new spirit was the Station Area Specific Plan (SASP), approved by the City Council on October 9, 2007 to guide development in the area roughly forming a half mile radius circle around the Railroad Station.

THE (REVOLUTIONARY) STATION AREA PLAN

What was so different about the SASP? For progressives, it promised to put Smart Growth principles to work rather than being simply noted as happened with the PMT Guiding Principles. Moreover, even strong supporters of the establishment growth machine like the late Bob Blanchard, who was Mayor at the time, understood the Plan's significance as the start of a fundamental reorientation away from highways. He called the SASP "a very big deal...the first transit-oriented development in Santa Rosa."[60]

The success of the SASP had much to do with the way political dynamics had shifted not only in Santa Rosa, but also in the region. For one thing, the basic SASP study was funded by a major grant from the regional Metropolitan Transportation Commission, which emphasizes transit-oriented development (TOD) and citizen participation in the planning process. MTC subsequently designated the SASP environs a Priority Development Area, enhancing the city's chances for development loans and grants. At the local level, the Accountable Development Coalition had come into being, pulling together diverse progressive interest to lobby for inclusionary housing, TOD and New Urbanist design principles. City planners mounted an extensive outreach program, and Santa Rosans turned out in numbers to make their views heard.

Complementing its TOD objectives, the SASP also struck new chords for urban design and land use priorities in Santa Rosa. Previous planning had much similar language, but generally assumed auto-centric projects and facilitated growth driven by developer investment. The SASP recognized that these factors remained critically relevant, but it shifted focus to emphasize neighborhood livability, pedestrian- and bicycle-friendly features, sustainable environment and preservation of open space. Not that implementation is a foregone conclusion – a smallish group of landowners in the Maxwell Court area just south of College Avenue belatedly appealed for a long-term exemption from rezoning. Mayor Gorin, despite her progressive credentials, lent a sympathetic ear to their special pleading, and as of early 2010, General Plan amendments to accommodate them were under active consideration.

The SASP also broke sharply away from developer influence with two critical departures from the previous approach to inclusionary housing. One change eliminated a policy which had exempted developers of mixed-use projects (i.e., a project which has both commercial and residential components) from requirements to provide for a certain percentage of affordable housing. Ostensibly intended to promote mixed-use development, this de facto benefit for developers was of doubtful impact and, presumably for that reason, has not been used by other cities. The other SASP housing policy change was one that in effect increased pressure on developers to build affordable housing units on the site of the project itself, as opposed to paying "in lieu" fees into a fund for constructing the units elsewhere.

The upshot of both new policies is to mandate a more "salt and pepper" mix of housing rather than splitting off affordable housing projects to place them in less desirable locations where land costs are lower. Developers charged that the changes will increase costs and result in fewer affordable units. That is probably true but only to a limited degree, and proponents of the changed approach argued successfully that any such downside was outweighed by the need to move away from the "ghettoization" implied by concentrating affordable housing in low-income areas. The SASP applies only to the area surrounding the Railroad Station, and developers along with construction industry representatives made a strong effort to prevent the new housing policies from being extended city-wide through the revisions for General Plan 2035. The new progressive majority on the Planning Commission held to the SASP model, although the Council wavered, pending a report back from a citizens' committee established by the Mayor to consider the Housing Allocation Plan, which in Ordinance form will implement any final Council-approved changes.

The new urban design thinking exemplified in the SASP strongly influenced other planning for the greater downtown area. A complementary Northern Linkages study has pointed the way to improve east-west connectivity along 7th and 6th Streets to cross Highway 101, a Mendocino Avenue Corridor Plan has been adopted for the stretch from College Avenue to Steele Lane, and a Santa Rosa Avenue Corridor Plan is in the works as of 2010 for that major thoroughfare from Sonoma Ave. south to Highway 12. All these plans involve efforts to move away from Santa Rosa's automobile-dominated streets and bleak parking lots to more visually appealing streetscapes, that are friendlier to bicycles and pedestrians, with trees, medians and more lively sidewalk activities. Cost and other factors, however, assure that implementation on the ground will not be easy or quick.

PEDESTRIANS AND BICYCLES

As the SASP was moving through stakeholder meetings in 2006, the City Council (then with a pro-developer majority) also bowed to pressure from local bicycle advocates and the Metropolitan Transportation Commission for greater attention to alternative transportation. It upgraded the Bicycle and Pedestrian Advisory Committee to a full-fledged city board with 9 members – seven appointed by Council plus representatives for seniors and disabled persons. The new Bicycle and Pedestrian Advisory Board (BPAB) promptly set about to promote better facilities for its constituency, in particular bicycle lanes. This involved a change in the planning culture of a city long reluctant to give up auto-centric thinking – one pro-developer Council Member was overheard in a supermarket queue to grumble about "Fountaingrove colleagues who seemed to want a bicycle lane on every street!"

Grumbles there were aplenty from such quarters, but on these themes, times were rapidly changing. The Sonoma County Bicycle Coalition (SCBC) evolved into a potent grassroots political machine, and meshed well with a host of like-minded activists and non-profit organizations. The Council on Aging in October 2006 got major attention with a "Take Back Our Streets" march and rally for bicycle and pedestrian safety. In 2008, Gary Wysocky, a founding member of SCBC, finished at the top of the list to win a seat on the City Council, and Shirlee Zane, who organized the Take Back Our Streets march, won a County Supervisor seat, upsetting Sharon Wright, a three-time former Santa Rosa Mayor and champion of growth.

> LEADERSHIP INSTITUTE FOR
> ECOLOGY & THE ECONOMY
> RICK THEIS AND TANYA NARATH
>
> The Institute's Mission: "Educating leaders to create public policy that is environmentally friendly, socially equitable and economically viable for a sustainable community."
> *****
>
> **Rick Theis** founded the Institute in 2000. While Executive Director of the Sonoma County Grape Growers Association, he had come to realize the need for better city planning and urban growth boundaries to not only protect ag land, wildlife habitat and open space, but also to address social justice and economic concerns. The Institute's seminar-style ten-month long course has a record of solid achievement in training current and future leaders – already over 100 hold or have held positions on city councils, boards and commissions.
>
> **Tanya Narath,** moved to the Institute after a career with HP and Agilent in information technologies. Executive Director of the Institute since December 2005, Narath has produced major educational programs on topics including Smart Growth and policies for a sustainable future.

THE TRICK IS SUSTAINABLE GROWTH

If transit-oriented-development and growth around SMART stations is good, what about satellite suburbs? In November 2009, a small group of landowners proposed that Santa Rosa begin planning for development of 420 acres east of Santa Rosa Ave. between Yolanda Ave. and Todd Rd. The area, lying outside the city limits, was included in the Urban Growth Boundary as drawn in 1996 with the stipulation that it not be developed and annexed before 2010 – that peculiar formulation was a compromise to assuage environmentalists who did not want the parcels included in the UGB at all

The proposal put on the table in 2009 presented itself as the very model of a New Urbanist community. It gave few details on specifics like amount and types of housing units, but it went to great lengths to assure the City the project would be sustainable in all respects, environmentally responsible, highly livable, walkable, etc. The developers undertook to pay all costs associated with initial environmental review, planning requirements and city staff work. Growth proponents were sure to applaud the project for the (temporary) construction jobs it would create, and the general addition to the City's economic activity.

But the downsides of the proposal are immediately apparent. In the first instance, there is no showing that such a project, mostly residential and distant from developed areas of the City, can pay its way to cover the associated costs for infrastructure and services. Annexation itself is also a major issue, given that other much more integral areas, notably part of Roseland, have been in line to come into the City, but have been stalled because of anticipated post-annexation drains on City coffers. There is, moreover, the overarching question of why the City should consider annexing a satellite development, when the major thrust of its development energies has been committed to the central areas of downtown and near-future SMART stations where transit-oriented-development and the connectivity to existing infrastructure and services promises the biggest pay-offs for sustainability and use of City resources.

Then too, broad questions of water supply, wastewater disposal, traffic congestion and open space must also be dealt with. To meet future water needs, more stringent conservation by all citizens is a virtually certain requirement, and many Santa Rosans resent the prospect of having to cut their water use permanently so that projects like this can be developed. Inevitably also, such a project would worsen traffic along already congested sections of Santa Rosa Ave., open space would be lost (the proposal notes it would seek to minimize "hard visible impacts to Petaluma Hill Road"), and wastewater system infrastructure is costly.

More projects lie ahead around the City's periphery and would raise similar issues. Though smaller, "Elnoka," a housing development proposal along Melita Rd. and Highway 12, just west of Oakmont, is also distant from transit and would burden already congested roads, although it has been stalled largely because of NIMBY concerns expressed by Oakmont residents. In the southeast, there are prospects for numerous projects to fill undeveloped areas along the foothills, and the City has plodded ahead with now dated and, many would say, very questionable plans to extend Farmer's Lane so that it can carry higher density traffic through the middle of that quadrant. And the many older suburbs, whether completely or only partially built-out are in need of retrofitting to reduce auto-dependency and adverse environmental impacts.

CHOICES AND POLITICS

What lies ahead on the planning front? Although recent events, such as adoption of the SASP and failure of traditional big-box store applications, have signaled a potential change in course, the outlook is still uncertain, and the planning framework provides for many options. As indicated above, there is considerable land that can yet be developed or redeveloped within the Urban Growth Boundary, and the City General Plan still looks to accommodate the 70,000 new residents projected to be coming Santa Rosa's way by 2035. As of 2010, in theory at least the overall question on the table is what are the conditions under which Santa Rosans will welcome growth to become a city of 233,000.

In Santa Rosa, the partisan divide will persist. Progressives want stronger assurances up front that growth will not entail cutting corners on environmental, social justice or quality of life issues for residents across the city. On the other side, the growth coalition described in earlier chapters remains intact, and collectively believes its interests will be best served by continued free-flowing growth and economic expansion, with city subsidies where necessary.

Future City Councils will have to make the decisions on priorities and the choices of projects that qualify for approval. The major test to be applied to upcoming development proposals will be "sustainability."

While the word is more frequently uttered by progressives, growth advocates are also keenly aware that they must demonstrate approaches that make sense for the long haul. What are the issues and principal decisions that lie ahead? And what does sustainability entail in this context? The next chapters take up in more detail the three challenges of sustainability – environmental, economic and social.

CHAPTER 10

THE ENVIRONMENTAL AGENDA – HOW GREEN, HOW FAST?

The now classic definition of sustainability dates from the 1987 report of a United Nations Commission on Environment and Development chaired by Norwegian Prime Minister Gro Harlem Brundtland: "Meeting the needs of the present generation without compromising the ability of future generations to meet their needs." Though initially presented with a strong environmental focus, the sustainability concept is now generally conceived to rest on three separate, but closely inter-related, "pillars" – the environment, economy and social equity. This chapter takes up Santa Rosa and the first pillar.

Any comprehensive index of environmental sustainability covers climate change, ecosystem vitality, resource conservation and environmental health. Santa Rosa is affected one way or another by all these concerns, but the two most prominent issues on the city's agenda as of 2010 involve reduction of greenhouse gases (GHG) and management of water. On the former, Santa Rosa signed on to the county-wide plan to reduce GHG emissions, and the City has a solid record of achievement in its own municipal operations. But the automobile continues to rule – ultimate success in reaching the GHG reduction targets requires a major reduction in vehicle miles traveled and that is highly unlikely without wholesale shifts in attitudes, urban design and development patterns.

As for water, strong doubts persist about the reliability of City and County water supply projections. The picture is complicated by rising costs, endangerment of salmon and threats of groundwater pollution. In addition to water issues, Santa Rosa environmentalists also remain concerned about sufficiency of parks, as well as maintaining the Urban Growth Boundary limits, hillside and ridgeline building restrictions, open space and habitat protections.

Santa Rosa will surely move toward greater environmental sustainability. But the tussles will continue between progressive and pro-developer political factions over how fast to do so, and where the priorities should lie. This chapter examines how Santa Rosa is coping with the environmental challenges and competing views of how best to proceed.

GHG REDUCTION --ACTION PLANS

SCEIP
(SONOMA COUNTY ENERGY
INDEPENDENCE PROGRAM)

-County loan program for energy efficiency
-For real property, e.g. add solar, insulation
-$100 million available, $40m applied (1/2010)
-Repayment through property tax bill over time
-Nationally acclaimed path-finding model

CCAP
(COMMUNITY CLIMATE ACTION
PLAN)

-Supports County/City GHG reduction goal
-Broad-based community report adopted 2008
-Four areas:
   -energy efficient retrofits (planning 1/2010)
   -transit, e.g., SMART, County Trans. Plan
   -renewable energy, e.g., SCEIP
   -conserve & capture, e.g., open space, waste

ps – a little guy: North Bay Eco-Workforce
Evelina Molina and Cris Oseguera

-shoestring grassroots non-profit
-home storm windows and gray water systems
-trains at-risk youth
-provides low-cost products and installations

TACKLING CLIMATE CHANGE – SERIOUSLY?

Santa Rosa and surrounding jurisdictions have been quick off the mark to recognize the need for action on global warming. In 2005 Santa Rosa, all other eight municipalities and the County resolved to meet the exceptionally ambitious target set by a county-wide Community

Climate Action Plan (CCAP) – the boldest in the nation – to reduce GHG emissions 25% below 1990 levels by 2015. The Plan was drawn up under the aegis of the local non-profit Climate Protection Campaign, led by Executive Director Ann Hancock with a range of technical experts and community advisers. In 2009, the State Legislature passed a special bill, AB 881 (Huffman), to create the Sonoma County Regional Climate Protection Authority (SCRCPA) to coordinate GHG reductions efforts, in particular the follow-on implementation of the CCAP's four major action categories: energy efficiency, smart transit and land use, renewable energy and conservation.

Of the four work areas, "smart transit" presents the greatest difficulties. The Plan notes that transportation accounted for about 60% of GHG emissions across the County in 2007 – nearly four out of five trips made here are by single-occupant fossil fuel-powered vehicles. The CCAP aims to cut GHG emissions from transportation by 588,000 tons of CO_2 below "business as usual," or 41% of the total savings needed to meet the 2015 target. To do that will require far less car and truck use, but the County's newly revised Comprehensive Transportation Plan (CTP), approved in 2009, has few teeth and, worse, endorses freeway widening projects that will induce more traffic. Willard Richards, Chair of the widely-respected citizen watchdog Sonoma County Transportation and Land Use Coalition could only conclude: "Implementing the 2009 CTP would prevent Sonoma County from achieving its 2015 climate protection goal in the foreseeable future."[61]

There seems no easy way to resolve the dilemma. The freeway projects have been in the works for years and have broad support from drivers plagued by maddening traffic congestion. But analysis of the projected CTP activities demonstrated that vehicle miles traveled in the County and hence GHG emissions would increase in the next few years, not decrease. On this topic, the irony is that the governing Board of the SCTA which approved the CTP has the same individuals as the Board of the Regional Climate Protection Authority charged to achieve reductions. Clearly, a radical new approach bringing all stakeholders together must be found if progress is to be made – as of early 2010, prospects were dim at best for success and much of all this is beyond the influence of the City, which has only one representative on the 10-person Sonoma County Transportation Authority Board.

On the more positive side, the largest potential contribution to GHG reductions under the CCAP would come from low carbon electricity development with 67% new local renewables. The CCAP goal here is a 630,000 ton reduction in CO2, or 45% of the plan target. Santa Rosa has signed on to the County's path-breaking $100 million Energy Independence Program (SCEIP), which was the first public energy improvement loan program under the California legislation (AB 811), which authorized financing programs for energy improvement projects on private property. The County has made $100 million in loans available to property owners to finance energy efficiency, water efficiency and renewable energy projects. The voluntary assessments are attached to the property, not the owner, to be paid back through the property tax system over time. SCEIP got off to a good start with loans of $23.9 million approved through mid-December 2009, even though the interest rate at 7% was a disincentive for some.

GREEN BUILDING – WORK IN PROGRESS

"Green building" refers to measures that reduce the adverse impact of buildings on the environment. It's a critical concept for GHG reduction since buildings account for about 40% of the energy consumed in the US. Good design and construction practice from siting to insulation can produce far more energy efficient new buildings and "retrofit" existing buildings to higher standards. Given that such measures involve at least some costs, governments like Santa Rosa's are faced with decisions on how high to set the bar and whether to make compliance mandatory. There is broad support for green building in Santa Rosa, when it comes to new construction, but consensus remains elusive on the issues of retrofitting existing structures.

The city is on track to implement higher standards for new buildings and should come smoothly into compliance with Calgreen, the stringent new California state code. The City Council took its first step in 2007, when it passed a mandatory Green Building Ordinance (GBO) for new construction. The point targets were not especially high, but the Council in February 2009 directed an increase. The bar will now likely be set to meet the Calgreen standards, the most strict of any State, which are to take effect on January 1, 2011.

Retrofitting for existing buildings is another matter. When the report of the City's broad-based Green Building Advisory Committee went before the Council in February 2009, the issues of what to do about retrofitting older buildings provoked especially acrimonious exchanges over their pocketbook implications. Up-front costs can be high for homeowners already pressed to meet mortgage payments, and the concept of requiring that standards be enforced at the time of sale ran into vociferous opposition from the local real estate community. As of early 2010, the options were still under consideration in City Hall.

Meanwhile, a parallel county program continued to evolve. The Climate Protection Campaign hired a consulting team and later joined with the County Climate Protection Authority noted above to "design and implement" a county-wide program to retrofit existing buildings to meet the GHG reduction goals adopted for the Community Climate Action Plan. The Plan called for retrofitting 80% of existing buildings to a relatively high standard by 2015 to achieve a GHG reduction of 168,000 tons of CO2, or 12% of the overall target. While program organizers hoped to get pilot projects underway by spring 2010, critics are skeptical that the 80% target can be achieved by 2015, given homeowner cost concerns and the lack of concrete progress through 2009. Separately, local contractors are marketing retrofit services and two non-profits have been developing programs with work opportunities for at-risk youth.[62]

SANTA ROSA MUNICIPAL OPERATIONS – GREEN AS GOLD

The City itself has made major strides to "green" its own operations. In 2009, the US Department of Energy named Santa Rosa one of only 25 Solar American Cities in the nation for its commitment to adoption of solar technology at the local level. The DOE website notes: "A leader in environmental conservation and clean technologies, (Santa Rosa) was placed at #5 in the nation's top ten green cities in National Geographic's Green Guide 2006."[63] Other national recognition includes an EPA award for clean water, and national awards for the Geysers Recharge Project and the Aquatic Biomass-to-Fuel Project.

There is more in the City's green tool box. Its vehicle fleet has a large number of hybrid and natural gas-powered vehicles; the transit system,

City Bus, has also begun adding hybrids; there is an Environmentally Preferred Purchasing program to buy green products where possible; and the City proactively supports green business programs, promotion of environmental protection for creeks and storm drains, and proper disposal of pharmaceuticals. Thinking green has become a part of City Administration culture, and that fact is testimony to the non-partisan support for environmental sustainability, at least for measures that can be taken directly by the city.

ENOUGH WATER? – SUPPLY DOUBTS AND ECOSYSTEM ISSUES

As of early 2010, the biggest water question for Santa Rosa was the most fundamental – will the city have an adequate supply to keep current residents going and support a projected population increase of 70,000 more through the General Plan period ending in 2035? The stock answer for nearly two decades has been "yes," based on the fact that the city's prime supplier, the Sonoma County Water Agency (SCWA), can count on ample quantities of water reserves in its Sonoma and Mendocino Lake storage facilities.

The catch is that it is not yet possible to get all that good water from the bigger Lake Sonoma to Santa Rosa taps. Because Dry Creek, the main channel that now carries water down from the lake, does not have adequate capacity, SCWA with the eager support of the City has been planning for the last 15 years or so to build a pipeline. The grand plan, known for short as the "Water Project," has been key for growth planning and kept on moving forward despite serious potential problems, in particular costs estimated at over $600 million; land rights; environmentalist opposition; and endangered salmon.

But the grand plan was killed in August 2009 after SCWA bowed to the demands of a federal "Biological Opinion" that imposed severe new restrictions on the use of Dry Creek. The Opinion, issued by the National Marine Fisheries Service in September 2008, requires SCWA to take steps to protect coho salmon, Chinook salmon and steelhead by better controlling Russian River and Dry Creek – the problem is that at different times of the year, either too little water or too much can spoil spawning or destroy habitat. Moreover, Dry Creek habitat must now be restored at a probable cost of $100 million or more. Federal or State grants may help, but ultimately the water users throughout Sonoma and Marin Counties will have to guarantee that costs are met to both implement requirements of the Biological Opinion and sustain the overall supply system.

When SCWA abandoned the Water Project, it advised customers like Santa Rosa to live within current allocations and meet additional future requirements from conservation measures, recycling and possibly groundwater. That changed the answer about adequacy of Santa Rosa's water supplies from "yes" to "maybe," and threatened to throw the city's forward planning into a cocked hat. The City tried to stop the SCWA from scrapping the Water Project, but lost its bid to get a judge to issue a Temporary Restraining Order. At that point in late September 2009, the SCWA formally withdrew its long-pending request to the State for more water allocations and said it would rely on some combination of existing supplies and 12 conservation-oriented "strategies" to meet future demand from customers including Santa Rosa and Marin County.

The short term (five-year) impact for Santa Rosa is apparently manageable, assuming no natural disasters such as extreme droughts or earthquakes. By its own Water Supply Assessment,[64] the city will have enough water from existing supplies to meet projected population growth through 2015, and could stretch to 2018 if it gave up plans

> ### JENNY BARD
> ### CLEAN AIR ADVOCATE –
> ### CIVIC ACTIVIST
>
> Even if Jenny Bard didn't work for the American Lung Association (she is the ALA's Regional Air Quality Director), she would be an energetic promoter of clean air and healthy living. Bard misses no opportunity to advance these causes, whether on the job with ALA, supporting local government and non-profit activities or initiating something on her own.
>
> Bard is also a strong advocate for community building with an exceptional track record of making a difference. In her Junior College neighborhood, she catalyzed grassroots action to make the streetscape and entry for a new college parking garage more bicycle and pedestrian friendly (see Chapter 6), and induced the City to make a planning study for the neighborhood's main thoroughfare and shopping area along Mendocino Ave.
>
> "Visionary leadership and community engagement," Bard says, are needed to push local government from process to policy for a sustainable future. Bard has more than done her part to move Santa Rosa in that direction.

to extend services to some neighborhoods now using well water. The problem there, however, is that the wells, if continued, might be subject to contamination from nearby sources.

The longer term outlook is much more uncertain. The Water Supply Assessment estimated that the City could meet future demand for the population growth projected in the General Plan by utilizing a combination of some increase from SCWA, implementation of a Water Recycling Project already designed, drawing additional groundwater and "stringent" conservation measures. When City authorities reevaluated the assessment to take out the previously anticipated SCWA increase, they still concluded that the remaining sources could provide adequate water to meet demand – although they did not offer much in the way of explanatory numbers.

The City's optimistic evaluation in any case has shaky assumptions. The availability of groundwater from wells, for example, has yet to be fully assessed. Although studies have indicated that the water table under the city has not significantly lowered over the last decade or more, the groundwater picture will not have a solid scientific basis until completion in late 2010 of a major study of the Santa Rosa plain. Meanwhile, exploratory drilling by the City in 2009 failed to identify good new well sites, and overall the soils encountered were not conducive for use of wells to extract groundwater.

Also, of course, Mother Nature holds trump cards. Old timers still remember the near catastrophic North Bay drought of the mid-1970s, and global warming could well mean considerably less average rainfall in future years than historical records would indicate. One probable new requirement to even out rainfall swings will be a major increase in storage capacity to hold the excess of winter water for summer use. That is one of SCWA's top new priorities for its customers, but it will be neither easy nor cheap to accomplish.

Use of recycled water is also high on the list of expandable sources, but the catch may be cost. Santa Rosa has had a recycle program since 1966, and as of 2010 produces over 20 million gallons per day of high-quality, tertiary-treated water that is safe for the irrigation of landscapes, agricultural crops, vineyards, playgrounds, golf courses, and parks. The City operates a sub-regional system including Rohnert Park, Sebastopol and Cotati; while also sending about half of the processed water to The

Geysers, where it is pumped into underground steam fields to generate electricity. But recycling systems cost money, and there is an estimated price tag of well over $120 million to phase in water recycling projects, which may be needed for "new" water to help cover the gap from SCWA's retreat.

Future cost is perhaps the biggest uncertainty – how much pain will city ratepayers be willing to bear? Santa Rosans have an excellent record of conservation to stretch limited water supplies, but they have long grumbled. As Press Democrat columnist Chris Coursey wrote in mid-2007, "I can't recall a single person I've talked to about this issue who hasn't wondered why, if all of us are being asked to conserve water, there's been no mention of a plan to stop -- or at least cut back -- the construction of new houses. Or condos. Or apartments, or office buildings, or casinos."[65]

Nonetheless, in late 2009, the City Council approved rate increases to take effect in January 2010 of 8% for water and 7% for sewer, with a second round of similar hikes to kick in in 2011. A partial rationale for the raises was that SCWA in April 2009 upped its charges for water by 19%, although passing on this charge to Santa Rosa consumers accounted for less than a quarter of the City rate increases approved for 2010/2011. The Santa Rosa Utilities Department said the total increases were essential not only to adjust to higher SCWA charges, but also to fund operational costs, infrastructure maintenance and rising debt service, all aggravated in part also because utilities fund reserves had been drawn down in recent years.

Coming on the heels of very successful summer 2009 consumer conservation efforts, the increase struck many residents as at best confusing, at worst outrageous. How is it, they asked that when we save water, we then have to pay more? The City tried hard to explain that when consumers use less water, the City collects less money and then it comes up short of funds needed for operations and maintenance. But the Utilities Department accounting practices make it virtually impossible for ratepayers to see how much of the money charged on their bills for water is actually used to buy water from SCWA and how much is used to help cover maintenance or debt service costs. Although ratepayers generally accepted the increases voted in 2009, the absence of clear explanations left uneasiness about further rate hikes and almost certainly undermined the rationale for future conservation programs.

Also, the question raised by Coursey about balancing conservation and building permits seemed to many still unanswered. As a practical matter as of 2010, however, this point had become temporarily moot with the virtual halt in new construction that followed the financial melt-down of 2008.

GREEN SPACE -- UGBS, PARKS AND HABITAT

As discussed in Chapter 8 above, Santa Rosa, in common with virtually all American cities, practiced urban sprawl as a way of life for years after WW II. Anti-sprawl forces eventually reached critical mass in the North Bay and Santa Rosa's ballot measure passed in 1996 with nearly a two-thirds majority to put the Urban Growth Boundary in place for twenty years until 2016. The 2009 General Plan update covers growth projected to occur within the total area encompassed by the UGB, not just within the smaller area defined by city limits. Against that background, groups inside and outside City Hall began weighing the desirability of a ballot measure to prolong the UGB term from 2016 to 2035 to put it in sync with the General Plan.

As for parks, Santa Rosa is surrounded by a reasonably generous belt of green and open space. The initiative of Santa Rosa's post-WW II mortgage magnate Henry Trione made possible the creation of Annadel State Park in 1971, when he catalyzed an extraordinary public and private effort to acquire the land, himself donating about $450,000 of the total $4.3 million eventual cost. Santa Rosa also benefits greatly from Sonoma County's designation of community separators. In order to prevent unbroken urbanized road corridors, the County has identified parcels to be kept as green space and maintain separation between Santa Rosa and the neighboring communities of Sebastopol, Windsor and Rohnert Park.

Within Santa Rosa city limits, the adequacy of parks and recreational facilities depends in some measure on where one lives. Howarth Park and Spring Lake next to Annadel are exceptionally popular with residents from all parts of town, but the complex lies on the eastern edge of the city, requiring an auto trip by residents from the west side. The southwest quadrant has relatively less park space than the other three, even though it is arguably the most needy because of the higher concentration of low-income residents and in places denser housing. In that area, City officials have moved ahead on park development and new land acquisition with work to start in 2010 on Airfield Neighborhood Park west of Fresno Avenue (after delays because of tiger salamander habitat concerns), and a probable new purchase, long sought by southwest neighbors, to save a large plot of old oaks in Roseland for parkland. All across the city, after many years of neglecting creek rehabilitation and development, the City has also made great strides over the last two decades, notably the Prince Greenway project spearheaded over his two terms in office by popular progressive Council Member Steve Rabinowitsh.

As of 2010, the Department of Recreation and Parks has

> ## JUDY KENNEDY
> ### ADVOCATE – ENVIRONMENT, ARTS & NEIGHBORHOODS
>
> Judy Kennedy, a Santa Rosa native and resident of historic Burbank Gardens neighborhood, gives high value to "pride of place" community building, sustainable living practices and civic participation. She herself puts continuous energy into advocacy on all three fronts.
>
> Promoting neighborhoods, Kennedy started in her own back yard by organizing Burbank Gardens residents. From there she went on to become a founding member and active participant in the Neighborhood Alliance and a catalyst for city planning to breathe life into the racetrack-like stretch of Santa Rosa Ave. that splits her neighborhood from Juilliard Park. In parallel with community building, she takes every opportunity to work for sustainability – exemplified by her ZAP electric vehicle -- and to promote the arts
>
> Kennedy's latest project as of early 2010 was the 563-foot long Maple Ave mural, fourth longest in the US, to grace the western edge of Burbank Gardens District and offset the monotony of a parallel freeway embankment. More generally, she promotes the arts as member of the Art in Public Places Committee and adviser to the city Arts District.

little flexibility, having been hard hit by the budget crunches following on the 2008 recession. More cuts seemed sure to come on into 2010/11, forcing reduced services and greater reliance where possible on fee increases and volunteer assistance. These budget issues challenge the Department to keep up facilities like Howarth Park, Senior Centers and swimming pools, which enjoy strong public support, as well as to respond to neighborhood groups seeking more small parks, better geographic balance, and easier access to neighborhood parks.

Habitat for the endangered California tiger salamander is a special concern within city limits. Once occupying the entire Santa Rosa plain, the striking black and gold-colored salamander had lost much of its habitat to development by the time it was first put on the endangered species list in 2003. In late 2005, federal authorities of the Bush Administration reduced the protected area from 74,000 to 21,000 acres, and a group of local government, building industry and environmentalists worked to develop a conservation strategy that among other measures would allow mitigating offsets whereby a developer could build on a piece of habitat land if an appropriate plot were set aside elsewhere.

This offset strategy was unsatisfactory to many and in any case was never finalized. In 2009, a lawsuit forced the Fish and Wildlife Service to re-designate the entire 74,000 acre plain as protected. This sounds huge, but in fact the protections only apply to the relatively limited number of places within the overall area where there are suitable habitats for the tiger salamander. While southwest Santa Rosa will be most directly affected, the full impact of the policy change will not be clear for a year or two. Overall, the wetland ecosystem in and around the city has sustained irreparable damage, and the Laguna de Santa Rosa Foundation is leading efforts to save "several unique rare and endangered species in need of recovery found only in this corner of the world."[66]

CLEAN ENOUGH? – WATER, AIR AND SOIL

Supply issues aside, the quality of water delivered to Santa Rosa homes is high, exceeding state and federal standards. The city's water from SCWA, is cleansed through an unusual and highly effective system which filters it naturally through sixty feet of riverbed gravel and sand. The relatively small amount of water now obtained from City wells is also of high quality, although some private wells within the urban area have been totally contaminated by past industrial uses nearby. Local water issue activists have expressed concern that groundwater supplies are in danger of becoming contaminated by the common practice of flushing unused pharmaceuticals down home toilets – a potential problem all across the country that merits urgent attention.

Santa Rosa and Sonoma County also have a generally good situation with respect to the air we breathe. The American Lung Association gives Sonoma County an A (very good) rating for ozone pollution and a B for particulate pollution. That does not, however, mean there are no serious problems. Perhaps most worrisome is pollution of air pockets around automobile concentrations – near main highways or around schools when parents drop off or pick up children. The elderly and children are vulnerable, and higher than average rates of asthma in students have been reported in some school districts in Santa Rosa. Ash and smoke from nearby forest fires can create problems, even from short exposure, as happened in the summer of 2008.

Underneath our feet, Santa Rosa has a number of contaminated soil pockets – known as brownfields – left from the days when few people worried about leakage from oil storage tanks or dumping of toxics fluids like those used in dry cleaners. If it disappeared into the soil, we thought that was the end of it. Dreadfully wrong, of course, and now sites like those formerly used for gas stations or industrial activities must be cleaned up, often at considerable cost, before they can be used. The Vineyard Creek Hotel, the entrance to the Prince Greenway, and the new Airfield Park in Southwest are all examples of land plots contaminated by poor past practice, which have had to be put right.

Payment for clean up is a major issue. For many polluted sites, liability may be impossible to establish or the responsible parties may have long since gone out of business. To help land owners stuck with a contaminated site, the City has secured a U.S. Environmental Protection Agency (EPA) Brownfields Cleanup Revolving Loan Fund (RLF) grant. The Brownfields RLF provides funding in the form of low-interest loans to address toxic contamination problems within the city limits.

LASTING CHANGE – THE IMPORTANCE OF URBAN DESIGN

For future development of US cities and towns, environmental sustainability has become an urgent task that can only be accomplished with a comprehensive response. A band aid, project-by-project approach will not bring change rapidly enough on the scale needed. In recognition of this, urban planners have for some time been working to address the larger picture with concepts such as transit-oriented development and "complete neighborhoods," but progress has been slow.

Much current thinking has been inspired by the "New Urbanist" movement, which emerged in the 1980s to counter urban sprawl. Its proponents set out architectural and aesthetic principles intended to capture the quality of life associated with city neighborhoods functioning at their best – diverse, vibrant, and quintessentially human.

Northern California played a seminal role when in 1991, the Local Government Commission (LGC), a non-profit in Sacramento, invited prominent architects and planners to articulate a new doctrine for land use. The group assembled by LGC produced the Ahwahnee Principles, so named because they were first presented to a conference of elected officials at the Ahwahnee Hotel in Yosemite National Park later that same year. Subsequently, in 1993, the architects involved founded the Congress for the New Urbanism (CNU), which has become the leading voice for the philosophy. The award-winning Local Government Commission (www.lgc.org) has also continued its work "to build livable communities," with a strong emphasis on resource efficiency. A set of Ahwahnee Principles for Economic Development was added in 1997 and one for Water in 2005, inspired in large measure by California's critical needs. Rohnert Park Council Member and local environmental leader, Jake Mackenzie is a Vice-Chair of the LGC Board of Directors.

For its part, the spin-off Congress of New Urbanism (CNU) has been actively "promoting walkable, neighborhood-based development as an alternative to sprawl." (See www.cnu.org.) CNU played a substantial role in developing the national LEED (Leadership in Energy and Environmental Design) standards for environmentally sustainable construction and has been expanding with chapters on both coasts as well as in the mid-west. It focuses on well-defined traditional neighborhood layouts featuring walkability, mixed-use development with neighborhood shops and housing diversity, connectivity of streets and increased densities to be highest at town centers and near transportation.

"Smart Growth" is similar to New Urbanism. It also had its beginnings in the reaction against urban sprawl, but evolved with stronger environmental roots and a more grassroots orientation. One of its leading exponents, Smart Growth America (www.smartgrowthamerica.

org), states the movement's central objective as "to support citizen-driven planning that coordinates development, transportation, revitalization of older areas and preservation of open space and the environment." The Sierra Club and Greenbelt Alliance are members of Smart Growth America.

"Smart Growth" principles have considerable flexibility. Collaboration with stakeholders – an important aspect of the movement – provides for adaptation to fit local circumstance. At the same time, no one, obviously, wants to be in favor of "dumb growth," so the term "smart growth" has been distorted or co-opted by many who favor reliance on market forces with minimal restrictions on traditional patterns of development. Acceptance of green building principles, for example, can be advanced as support for Smart Growth even as other principles are de-emphasized or ignored.

Both Smart Growth and New Urbanism involve innovative approaches that can be difficult to implement on any major scale. Americans remain dependent on their cars, mass transit is only slowly expanding, and retrofits of whole communities involves great cost. Also, developers and their financiers are often unwilling to take risks, for example, by giving up reliance on a facilities such as free parking, that encourage use of personal cars.

THE POLITICS OF IT ALL IN SANTA ROSA

What does it all add up to in Santa Rosa? How green is the city, and is it giving environmental sustainability due weight? The answers depend on how one scores the report card on the performance discussed above in this chapter.

First, it must be said, Santa Rosa is very green by national American standards. The National Resources Defense Council (NRDC) ranked the city as second among medium-sized (pop. 100,000 – 249,999) municipalities across the nation.[67] The NRDC criteria include environmental standards, energy conservation, air and water quality, recycling, green building and standard of living. The EPA Solar Cities and National Geographic Green Guide recognition noted above add credibility to Santa Rosa's high standing as a candidate for anybody's top ten in its size category.

Whether Santa Rosa is doing as well as it should, however, is another matter. The answer to that kind of question depends on values and expectations. The city has not yet, for example, put in place the kind of mechanisms that have been established in Boulder, Colorado, Portland, Oregon or Seattle, where city-wide infrastructure has been developed with strong neighborhood participation. In Santa Rosa, Mayor Gorin initiated plans for a Sustainability Taskforce soon after her election at the end of 2008, but one year on, as of early 2010, it had yet to take hold.

Many environmentalists and their progressive soul-mates believe Santa Rosa should be doing better. They point to slowness in implementing a tough green building ordinance, hesitancy to come to grips with water supply realities, continued pressures for an auto-dependent downtown development model, and passive acceptance of plans for widened highways. Many who voice such criticisms want Santa Rosa to be more of a genuine leader, with government that would unequivocally adopt a mission as forceful and clear, for example, as the one articulated by the Sierra Club "to practice and promote the responsible use of the earth's ecosystems and resources."

Other Santa Rosans, however, say the city is already giving adequate or more than priority to the environment. They cite the national recognition noted above, but perhaps more to the point, they often argue that accelerating the city's current pace is unwarranted and risky for the city's overall well-being. The most vocal proponents of this assessment are local developers and construction industry representatives, whose views are reflected in the Sonoma County Alliance's mission statement, which sets its priorities as "to protect private property rights, to encourage a healthy economy, to maintain a sound environment..." pretty much in that order.

Despite the general acceptance of priorities like GHG reduction and wide-spread business support for green industry, there is still a fault line between growth adherents and progressives. The divide has been manifest whenever difficult development decisions came before the City Council, notably when growth proponents supported a big box store (Lowe's) because of its possible, albeit not certain, sales tax income; or when construction industry representatives fought for approval of a senior apartment complex (Fountaingrove Lodge) despite adverse environmental impact.

Such factionalism continues to bedevil the debate in Santa Rosa over sustainable development. Whether driven by economic self-interest or ideological conviction, leaders from growth coalition circles have spoken out with a sharp emotional and political edge that seemed intended to frame the local election agenda for November 2010.

Chapter 13 will take a closer look at how all this will be affected by elections in 2010 and beyond. Before that, the next two chapters examine the other pillars of sustainability – the economic and the social.

CHAPTER 11

A Sustainable Economy – What Does It Mean for Santa Rosa?

The Great Recession of 2008 threw the local economy into a severe tailspin. As of early 2010, most experts seem to think our corner of the world will recover over the next two or three years, but it will likely be a slow uphill climb, and what comes next won't be the same as what went before.

What can the City administration do? Local governments are largely at the mercy of national trends, but cities do have some tools and Santa Rosa has pulled them together in an Economic Sustainability Strategy. Downtown's future remains problematic with a disunited business community, even as the new Gateways Redevelopment Project is poised to infuse additional funding into the city center. The County's role is also significant, although the sensible notion of regional coordination on key issues like tax sharing remains a distant dream.

The City budget is struggling to stay solvent – a true sustainability problem! It is caught between unstable revenues and the kind of escalating costs, notably for personnel, that bedevil cities across the state. Deep staffing and service cuts are inevitable, and user fees, including those for utilities, are also escalating.

The City Council is searching for a better "triple bottom line" – balancing economic with environmental and social equity needs. This chapter examines the major assessments and ideas on the table, and what is being considered to cope with post-2009 economic realities.

A SUSTAINABLE ECONOMY – JUST WHAT IS IT?

The phrase "sustainable economy" is an over-used, often ill-defined term. In the original context of international efforts to stop development that was rapidly degrading the planet's environment, it means essentially an economic system in which resources are not used up faster than nature renews them. But life gets more complicated when one considers the full range of inter-relationships between the economy, society and the environment, the above-mentioned three pillars of sustainability. That thinking has given rise to the concept of the "triple bottom line," defined for an individual company as "financial, social, and environmental effects of a firm's policies and actions that determine its viability as a sustainable organization."[68]

In Santa Rosa, the 2008/9 recession has focused attention in the first instance on how to energize the local economy. That involves promotion of competitiveness, innovation and infrastructure to attract new enterprise, as well as to keep the existing base going. There are high hopes for development of green industries, but that will take time even with the exceptional support from local city/county programs.

A sustainable economy is also of course essential to the health and capacity of the city's government. Sales, property and other taxes provide well over half of the money for the City's discretionary spending, which includes police, fire, public works, parks and recreation. Budget shortfalls are posing difficult problems, and in real life, Santa Rosa like most cities is not the master of its financial fate, since it is powerless to influence the swings of the national economy and can be hostage to state and federal actions.

AFTER THE KILLER RECESSION

As 2009 closed out, Santa Rosa and the surrounding area remained in the grip of a persistent national economic recession, even though it was technically over with recovery underway. Unemployment in the county still hovered around 10%, crop income was down, evictions and foreclosures continued to rise, the median home price had dropped by near 40%, the City budget was crippled by falling tax revenues, new housing permits had plummeted and local retailers struggled to stay in business. Some old mainstays were down significantly, led by the construction industry, with retail trade not far behind, while tourism agriculture and wealth management registered significant declines. Only the health and wellness sector had been managing a small job growth locally, according to a June 2009 Moody's Economy.com report.[69]

Other reports show a similar mixed bag – it's going to get better, they say, but not very quickly. ABAG's January 2010 report[70] said the North Bay will remain "mired in the hole," with unemployment hovering around 10% – but that's still the ninth lowest unemployment rate of California's 58 counties. The County Economic Development Board's 2010 preliminary Indicators

COUNTY ECONOMIC REPORT FEB. 2010
Projections – recession will bottom in 2010
-Gross metro product: 2010 - $17.7 bil. 2012 - 19.6
-Unemployment: 2010 - 10.8% 2012 - 8.1%
Winter 2010 stats: -Cost of living 2010 (US=100) 145% -Cost of doing business (US=100) 98%
Economic strengths -household wealth = credit strength -increasing net migration (2010: +4,000)
Economic weaknesses -costs to basic & office-using industries -increasing pipeline of foreclosures
Top employers: Local Gvt: 23,976; State: 4,912; Fed: 1,702; Kaiser: 2,400; Sutter: 1,781; St. Joseph: 1,097; Safeway: 1,082; Agilent: 1,050
Source: Sonoma County Economic Development Board

Report[71] talked of a mix of "needs and opportunity." On the negative side, jobs were still being lost and unemployment had increased, the poverty rate was up 2% from 2007 to 2008, and hotel occupancy was down. In the plus column, housing affordability had nearly doubled, new businesses had continued to emerge, and where there had been job growth over the last decade, wage levels had been above average. All in all it could have been worse, and it looks to be getting better, but not very fast.

For the future, as of early 2010, experts are cautiously optimistic with predictions for an upturn kicking in by 2011/12. In an October 2009 presentation[72] sponsored by the Sonoma County Economic

Development Board Foundation, well-known analyst Christopher Thornberg opined there was no "fast recovery" in the offing. For the longer run, Thornberg was "bullish" on California, citing the State's economic resiliency over the last 15 years and the benefits of the drop in housing prices. In the earlier June 2009 review mentioned above, Moody's analysis dealt more specifically with Sonoma County, and also was comparatively upbeat: "the county's various food, beverage and tech-producing industries will expand, supplemented by a travel and tourism industry with broader offerings toward health and lifestyle, and a workforce that is highly skilled and innovative." More generally on the positive side, Santa Rosa retains many advantages as a desirable location – its climate, natural beauty, nearness to San Francisco, sound infrastructure and well-educated population all bode well as and when the economy picks back up.

The bad news is that many local businesses and individuals were battered throughout the Great Recession and may not be able to hold out for the up-tick. At the high end of the financial disaster scale, in October 2009 the county's largest landowners, Clem and Anne Marie Carinalli, were forced into bankruptcy court, unable to cover repayments for $150 million in loans. Three local branches of large-stores – Mervyns, Gottschalks and Circuit City – went out of business, and a local icon – downtown Sawyers News – announced it would have to shutter the doors in mid-2010, its profits squeezed by the recession on top of competition from nearby national book retailer, Barnes and Noble. And more local foreclosures seemed likely to follow under pressure from employment losses and continuing tight credit. Nearly one in three mortgage holders in Sonoma County was reported at the end of 2009 to be "under water," owing more on their house than the property was worth.[73]

SANTA ROSA'S ECONOMIC SUSTAINABILITY STRATEGY

It's easy to overstate what any local government can do to promote economic activity on its own territory. Although city administrations everywhere talk up their "job creation" programs, by and large, broader economic forces are what fuel employment growth, and local authorities are secondary players, competing with each other to attract new business and the jobs that come with it. Local governments can of course create jobs directly by hiring new employees, but beyond that, overall payroll employment has generally followed business cycles, independent of local government policies, for both the short and long terms.

Local governments do, however, have tools at their disposal to affect where jobs will go. For starters, aggressive promotion and advertising can give potential employers a fuller appreciation of a city's competitive advantages in quality of life factors, sometimes more important to potential start-ups than local government policies – for example, weather, quality of life aspects and access to national transportation networks. In many situations, however, the decisive factors are pro-active measures that a local authority can cobble together to convey a positive business climate, including start-up or relocation assistance, accelerated issuance of business permits and/or fee reductions, good data on local markets and costs, inventories of location advantages, and customized attention to a prospective client's interests and needs.

Santa Rosa has in fact been playing this competitive game with vigor. In April 2008, the City adopted an Economic Sustainability Strategy (ESS),[74] building on a Strategic Plan developed in 2005 by Chabin Concepts under a consulting contract with the City. Chabin recognized that "City efforts can only set the stage for business investment and job creation. However," the consultants continued, "proactive leadership in economic development can foster long term results in cultivating an environment that welcomes business." To achieve these goals Chabin recommended a two-pronged approach: 1) create jobs and 2) grow local spending.

The *job creation* half of the effort has a strong focus on use of existing resources:

--maintain and grow existing businesses
--attract new businesses to existing employment centers
--maintain and enhance entrepreneur environment
--continue infrastructure improvements, in particular adaptive reuse of buildings

The *grow spending* half concentrates on the following elements:

--attract visitors with tourist promotion and focus on quality dining

--promote downtown, especially the "live, work, play" vision for development
--promote retail with "shop at home" campaign, market studies, under-used sites
--continue the downtown Arts District and promote arts & culture

Moving into 2010 with some recovery underway, the City Administration, Chamber of Commerce and most local business leaders continued to support the ESS. The City's dynamic new Economic Development Manager, Danielle Surdin O'Leary worked to carry it forward with more specific steps, such as updating the basic concepts, developing information packages, applying best practices and following up on implementation.

The ESS proposals themselves are hardly earthshaking. They do, however, give the sense of cohesion and direction needed for any development strategy. The Department of Economic Development has used its staff and the City's IT resources to pursue the ESS objectives by "offering guidance with finding available business space and starting... business, a one-stop permitting process, business tax certificates, and easy access to Economic Development, Community Development, and Advance Planning staff. In addition, we have established collaborative partnerships with key business players."[75] The Department also participates aggressively in regional and national conferences on business development and location.

On the ground, the City has made support of local business a priority in line with the Chabin proposals. The list of City programs through 2009, for example, is substantial: activities to draw shoppers downtown, from special events to the summer Wednesday Night Market; police resources devoted to a bicycle patrol and police substation on Courthouse Square; cooperation with GoLocal of Santa Rosa and other 'buy local' programs; discount parking coupon arrangements for downtown businesses; support for development of the Arts District (a specific recommendation of not only Chabin, but also the Mayors' Institute on City Design); and funding of the Convention and Visitors Bureau (CVB), working closely with it to attract conferences and the wildly successful Amgen Tour of California, which has featured world-class bicycle racers like Lance Armstrong and Santa Rosa's own Levi Leipheimer.

Much of the City's attention is focused on downtown as an important key to the city's economic well-being. City brochures call it "one great downtown – three distinct shopping districts," referring to the areas of Railroad Sq., Courthouse Sq. and the Plaza Mall. On the west side of the highway, Railroad Square merchants and property owners have long worked together as a group to promote its businesses, with considerable success. In the middle, the Plaza Mall has been something of an island, self-contained and profitable for its national chain owners, the Simon Property Group, headquartered in Indianapolis.

On the Courthouse Square side of downtown, merchants have relied more on City-supported interventions. City seed money enabled the start-up of Santa Rosa Main Street, a non-profit business association to foster economic activity downtown. From the beginning, the idea was that Main Street would soon transform itself into a self-financed business association, but dissenting business and property owners killed that possibility when they declined to support a Business Improvement District. In 2009, under severe budget pressures, the City ceased its subsidy, and Main Street closed its doors. The Chamber of Commerce, often criticized in the past for indifference to downtown, has shown a higher level of interest under its newly-hired President/CEO, Jonathan Coe, and may take up some of the slack left by Main Street's demise. As of early 2010, however, there was no visible indication that businesses and property owners were interested in organizing an association of Courthouse Square establishments.

SANTA ROSA REDEVELOPMENT AGENCY

California law authorizes cities like Santa Rosa to establish redevelopment agencies to help revitalize deteriorated or blighted areas, drawing on public funds to do so. The "blight" requirement for redevelopment eligibility often causes confusion since by common sense definitions, properties covered may appear to be in good shape. The basic idea is indeed that redevelopment applies to areas that have become blighted, like a slum, or abandoned industrial property, or a "dump" – the concept, however, has expanded so that it applies not only to physical dilapidation, but also to social or economic liabilities created by conditions such as substandard buildings or uses that have become incompatible with surroundings built later.

Redevelopment agencies do not levy or increase taxes. They collect "tax increments," meaning the incremental increase in tax collections that follow when a redevelopment area is improved such that property values go up or business activity produces more taxable income. The agencies can also borrow money in advance, to be repaid as and when the taxes rise from land improvements over time. Redevelopment funds are typically partnered with private capital, to provide "gap" funding, rather than used to undertake stand-alone government projects. By law in California, 20% of the tax increment must go to support affordable housing programs.

Santa Rosa has an active Redevelopment Agency with five project areas. The oldest, dating from 1961, covering a rough L-shape chunk of downtown including the Plaza Mall and City Hall across to E Street, played a major role in rebuilding downtown after the 1969 earthquake. The Grace Brothers project area generated what is now the Hyatt Hotel and Conference Center, and the Transit Oriented Redevelopment Project Area (TORPA) supports revitalization of the area to the west of the tracks in Railroad Sq., looking ahead to SMART train proposals. With a quite different focus, the Southwest Redevelopment area covers two large tracts of poorly developed land well south of Highway 12, with support for capital public improvements such as new and improved roads, parks, and sewer and water systems.

The fifth and newest area – the Gateways Redevelopment Project Area – will be critical for Santa Rosa's future development and its transition to sustainable city-centered growth. It covers considerable territory with a large section running north-south on the west side of Highway 101 from Third St to past Steele Lane, sections of near-downtown from well east of Brookwood to E and along the south side of College Avenue, plus large chunks by the railway near Coffey Lane and south of Hwy 12 to the east of Hwy 101. Gateways project funding will thus be available for such vital new activities as the rejuvenation of the area around Coddingtown Mall, development related to the two SMART stations proposed for Santa Rosa (Railroad Square and a new one at or near Jennings Avenue), the Santa Rosa Avenue corridor, downtown and a host of potential Transit-Oriented-Development projects along both the railroad and highway.

Gateways Redevelopment only got started as of October 2009, after being held up for over two years by a contrarian lawsuit. The losing case was filed in the name of Kay Tokerud, who, judging from press commentary, objected principally to the possibility that the City might invoke eminent domain powers. In the end, the suit reportedly cost the City several hundred thousand dollars and delayed redevelopment funding, but otherwise did not change the project's parameters. The case had nothing to do with the divide between pro-developer and progressive factions – the City's legal defense was supported formally by the Chamber of Commerce and informally by neighborhood residents. With the lawsuit decided and money starting to flow, the Chamber's Executive Vice President, Chris Lynch, called the Gateways Project "the engine of Santa Rosa's future."[76]

ENTER THE COUNTY AND REGIONAL BODIES

The County is a critical partner for the City in the promotion of economic activity. Infrastructure for water supply and transportation other than city streets is in the hands of the county, which also collects taxes, administers many health and welfare services; runs the library; and oversees numerous recreational facilities, parks, and open spaces. Its Economic Development Board (EDB)[77] fulfills two major functions: services to help local businesses, and the collection of information on significant economic activities, trends and projections for Sonoma County, such as the Indicators Reports noted above in this chapter.

What's good for local wine and tourism is good for Santa Rosa – perhaps the most prominent direct assist to the City comes from the Sonoma County Tourism Bureau (SCTB). The city's own Convention and Visitors Bureau works closely with SCTB to market the wine country in all its facets. It is an impressive tourist draw, in the words of the SCTB: "More than 250 wineries. Quaint towns. Crashing surf. Luxurious spas. Towering redwoods. Mystical rivers. Just 30 miles from San Francisco." Much of the tourist flow comes through Santa Rosa, although arguably the city could do better to capitalize on the trade, even though somewhere along the line it lost out to Windsor which got there first to trademark the slogan "Gateway to the Wine Country."

The County took the lead in 2009 to establish and implement a break-through energy improvement program, authorized under pioneering State legislation (AB 811). The Sonoma County Energy Improvement Program (SCEIP) pulled together a $100 million funding package to finance energy efficient property improvements, such as solar panels or insulation. The county pays the up-front cost of the improvements, and the property owner repays the county as an assessment on the property tax bill over a 5, 10, or 20 year period. Santa Rosa was quick to sign on and support the effort on a county-wide basis, rather than trying to mount its own program.

In 2007, the County established an Innovation Council of local community leaders to develop a strategic plan for improving the economy. The Council's final report, issued in early 2009, emphasized broad-based cooperation to promote resource efficiency, support innovation and develop the workforce. The last mentioned item, referring primarily to the county's growing Hispanic population, was perhaps the most significant of the Council's findings in that it helped call attention to the need for educational attainment, skilled workers and improved standards of living for this group. The Innovation Council's report offered little by way of new ideas to achieve this, however, and the advancement of the Latino community remains a major challenge for local government at both City and County levels.

REGIONAL BENEFITS ...AND PRESSURES

Finally, on the regional level, the nature and volume of Santa Rosa's economic activity also hinges on the engagement of two major regional bodies: MTC (the metropolitan Transportation Commission) and ABAG (the Association of Bay Area Governments). Working with both these bodies helps create a meaningful planning framework and keeps the City eligible for substantial funding from State and federal sources to underwrite projects that link into the regional picture, most obviously transportation, environment and housing.

ABAG is often cited by local officials as a kind of slave driver, forcing the City to accommodate more people than it wants and build more low income housing than it can afford. There may be some truth in this version, but Santa Rosa and Sonoma County developers have seemed very comfortable with the pro-growth pressures if not the affordable housing requirements. In any case, aside from the issue of whether it drives growth or just projects numbers (see Chapter 9 above), ABAG plays an essential role in regional coordination of transportation, housing, environmental protection, earthquake preparedness and equity issues. ABAG has a number of not so well known but very valuable programs, including work on a 500 mile shoreline trail system on public lands, conservation of the San Francisco estuary, standards for firms in environmental areas, a clearinghouse for federal grants, and hazard/risk information for earthquake preparedness. (The County and Cities name representatives to ABAG, with Mayor Gorin serving for Santa Rosa in 2009/10.)

Like ABAG, MTC has also evolved into a powerful regional influence. It has extensive authority to determine the mix of systems and priorities for development of regional transportation – and to channel federal and state funding for these purposes. Aside from mega projects like BART and regional highways, it also reaches down to the local level, where in Santa Rosa for example, it funded the Station Area Specific Plan and recently provided a grant for planning of the Santa Rosa Avenue Corridor from Courthouse Sq. to Highway 12. The attraction of "free" money can lead cities to shape their policies to fit the criteria for grant awards, although generally this has not been a problem between Santa Rosa and MTC, since both have adopted similar approaches with such priorities as Transit-Oriented-Development and Community Based Planning. (Sonoma County has one Commissioner to represent the County and all its cities, a position filled as of January 2010 by Rohnert Park City Council Member Jake Mackenzie.)

THE CITY BUDGET

City budgets across California are heavily dependent on brisk local economic activity. Sales and property taxes provide major infusions into Santa Rosa's General Fund, which pays for police and fire departments, public works, parks, recreation facilities and general administration. When local sales or property values dip, Santa Rosa has to scramble to cover on-going personnel and operational costs, which do not go down just because the economy is having a rough patch. (Water, sewer, parking and city bus services on the other hand are sustained by user fees – they are insulated to a large degree from short-term economic downturns, but the income from these "enterprises" cannot be transferred to cover General Fund shortfalls.)

The 2008 recession and the ongoing flat recovery through at least 2010 produced a crisis for the City's budget. Sales tax revenues fell for an unprecedented nine straight quarters through 2009, and even though City officials had been projecting a near worst case, the totals kept coming in below estimates to force ever deeper expenditure cuts. The City had prudently slashed expenditures for the FY 2009/2010 budget, but its chief financial officer, David Heath, told the Press Democrat that he expected the "financial woes will get considerably worse after the 2010-11 fiscal year unless the

GOLOCAL SONOMA COUNTY
THE POWER OF THE MULTIPLIER

For every $1 spent at a local business, $.45 stays local – for every $1 spent at a national chain store, $.15 stays local.

****

GoLocal is a "network of locally-owned businesses, citizens, non-profit organizations, and government agencies working together to build a resilient, thriving, local economy by supporting local, independently owned businesses and promoting sustainable practices."

GoLocal was formed as a cooperative in Santa Rosa in 2008 with about 25 founding member businesses. By the end of 2009 it had added 125 business , 90 individual and 10 organization members.

In addition to programs for education about and marketing of locally-owned enterprises, GoLocal has organized a rewards coupon program, a holiday sales campaign, and resource sharing by small businesses. Its activities have been paralleled by the City's Shop Santa Rosa promotional program.

Kelley Rajala is GoLocal's Executive Director.

economy improves," and the deficit threatened to go as high as $13.1 million by 2013-14, "if cuts aren't made along the way."[78]

Local government revenue recovery always lags behind when a recession moderates. So despite some overall economic promise, the City finds itself facing a grim budget picture, almost no matter what happens in 2010/11/12. As Heath noted, the City will be caught in the scissors of continued revenue shortfalls on the one side and increased expenditures on the other when deferred employee pay and other band-aid measures taken earlier will have to be set right. The math adds up to what accountants call a "structural deficit," meaning that if and when revenues return to "normal," there will still not be enough revenues to cover on-going city expenditures unless permanent cuts are made to programs and services, including reorganizations for efficiency of operations, reevaluation of pay and benefit scales, and thinning out of top-heavy management.

All this is made worse by California's financial system, routinely described as "dysfunctional" by economists of every political stripe. In California, it is not only exceedingly difficult for local governments to balance budgets on their own, but they are also at the mercy of raids on their treasuries when Sacramento wants funds for the State budget. On the revenue side, State constitutional amendments, including one submitted by Assemblywoman Evans, are under consideration for the 2010 ballot. On the expenditure side, state-wide consensus is also a necessary precondition if personnel costs are to be reined in by such measures as capping pension benefits. Without state-level reforms, Santa Rosa and Sonoma County can only do so much on their own either to increase revenues by seeking additional taxes and fees, or to reduce expenditures by asking their own employees to take less than norms prevailing in comparable locales. Cities, in common with many citizens have lobbied legislators hard for relief and proposed constitutional amendments to enable more sensible budgeting, but all such efforts to find ways out of the box have thus far gone nowhere.

Santa Rosa officials in fact did better than many city administrations to anticipate the financial crisis that burst upon them in 2008/9. With help from some city employees willing to defer pay raises and vigorous cuts, they were able to maintain a core level of services and programs. The City vigorously pursued federal economic stimulus funds, with some success in the transportation and housing sectors, maintained capital improvement projects wherever possible and supported activities such as the promotion of tourism and buy local campaigns.

The budget has been less of a political issue than it might appear. The pressure to cut has been so great and the choices so limited that all Council Members have had to go along with staff-recommended surgery for most of their key decisions. There has been tension between what amounts to conservatives and liberals in the community, for example over spending for public safety vs. for social programs or City civilian staff cuts, but compromises carried the day through the 2009/10 budget at least. Whatever happens in actual Council votes, budget rhetoric can of course always be useful in political campaigns, as was the case in 2008 when the pro-developer slate promised to make the "tough" decisions, without providing specifics.

THE BALANCE – GROWTH VS. SUSTAINABILITY

There is in theory room within the Urban Growth Boundary to accommodate the additional 70,000 residents projected by ABAG and accepted in the City's own General Plan. Many environmentalists are deeply concerned, however, that growth near that scale will overtax the environment and unacceptably deplete open space and water supplies. And in any case, the North Bay area's recent building boom followed by the crash has generated large commercial/industrial vacancy rates and left many residential properties "under water" – whether and how quickly new construction will pick up is problematic.

For the City, meeting infrastructure and service costs for future development will present major difficulties. Large development projects as a rule, and residential development projects in particular, do not generate enough revenue to pay for the improvements and additions to meet the needs of new residents. Even if development impact fees are greatly increased, there are questions of how much new development the City can support in the years ahead, given the projected slow recovery and rising costs of City services, especially for public safety.

These kinds of problems are less acute in and around the city center. The basic infrastructure is largely in place and city services can more easily be provided around the center, but already built-up suburban areas present an uneven picture. Bennett Valley/Montgomery Village, for example, is generally well served in most respects and Rincon Valley is well-established, but more recent, partially developed areas in southwest and northwest are still trying to catch up in such categories as parks and recreation facilities, availability of public transit, and public safety coverage.

In short, the economic dimension of sustainability has also taken on new meaning for cities like Santa Rosa. The combination of flagging revenues and increasing costs will likely make it ever more difficult for the City to both cover on-going services and accommodate new development, although federal and state grants will help for transit-oriented projects and others that advance sustainability objectives. Even the most optimistic projections do not suggest a stable, robust budget picture for the foreseeable future.

The next chapter takes up the third pillar of sustainability – social issues and how they relate to the environmental and economic parts of the sustainability equation.

CHAPTER 12

SOCIAL SUSTAINABILITY – THE THIRD LEG OF THE STOOL[79]

'Social sustainability' is fuzzy jargon, but it is a useful starting point to provoke thinking about – as Boulder, Colorado puts it – "how to make our community and city government more welcoming to, and inclusive of, all residents." In discussions of government policy, the phrase is typically used to add a human needs category to round out the more concrete economic and environmental concepts of sustainability.

In Santa Rosa, a number of pressing issues fall under the "social sustainability" rubric. They include: citizen engagement, inclusivity, services for seniors and youth; affordable housing requirements; and heritage preservation. Demographic changes are bringing higher proportions of Latino and senior residents – better integration of our Latino community is at or near the top of almost everyone's agenda for needed social change.

Building a more inclusive community with better social services is a daunting task for any city, and the financial capacity to help is limited. Many fine public and private programs have long been in place to tackle social problems in the city and county. Most are focused on specific areas, and there is an impressive overall track record of accomplishment. Nonetheless, significant numbers of our citizens remain under-served and under-represented – greater citizen engagement in government is a precondition for improvement.

If Santa Rosa is to work better for all its citizens in the 21st century, social sustainability must be addressed on par with its economic and environmental counterparts. The following pages explore how well Santa Rosa is doing.

SOCIAL SUSTAINABILITY – DOES SANTA ROSA HAVE IT?

The notion of social sustainability – and an appreciation of its importance – follows directly from the concepts of a sustainable environment and economy. Social development is the third leg of the stool, since the other two objectives cannot be achieved if the basic needs of the populace remain unmet. The economy for example needs a well-trained, well-fed, well-paid and well-housed workforce to continue strong performance. And caring for the environment is hardly possible without the participation of an educated and supportive citizenry that accepts the need to do so.

At the same time, communities struggle to define a manageable approach to social problems. Each city and town has a different mix of challenges, many of which can be politically sensitive, seemingly intractable, and/or beyond budget capacities to deal with them. Efforts to simply describe the issues often lead to long laundry lists, platitudes and impracticable demands for local resources. Nonetheless, at the end of the day, no city can avoid making collective decisions to establish distribution of resources for social needs, set priorities for environmental protection, make choices between development and open space, promote economic activity, and allocate municipal funds.

Santa Rosa has been relatively successful in coping with the social challenges endemic to mid-sized American cities: helping the homeless and poor; creating opportunity for seniors and youth; fighting crime; and combating discrimination. The city's well-to-do and charitable private sector has taken the lead to assist the needy and provide services from homeless shelters to Little League baseball diamonds. The City government has also had a number of supporting programs, aided until the recent economic crash by the North Bay's favorable economic situation. Now, however, the community finds itself running hard just to stay even, as cumulative economic difficulties have compounded the burdens for both the public and private sectors.

There is, moreover, a serious legacy of class and ethnic partition. In the frank words of one middle school principal, Santa Rosa is "a segregated city and … our children attend segregated schools."[80] The reference is to the fact that Elsie Allen High School and other schools in the Southwest are heavily Latino in comparison with schools in the other parts of the city. Much of the division can be ascribed to "market forces," as new workers, primarily Latinos moved in to fill lower-paying jobs and gravitated to the lower-cost housing, which for years has been most readily available to the west of Highway 101 and in the southwest of town. Growth machine-dominated City Councils generally did not see this as a problem and to some degree facilitated the trend by housing policies that favored putting new affordable housing projects on inexpensive land that already had a high percentage of minority residents.

Much of social sustainability, however, has to do with attitudes and political will. Broadly speaking, Santa Rosans recognize a need to do more to promote citizen engagement, diversity, and inclusivity, but there is not a strong consensus on how serious such shortcomings might be or how best to tackle them. Despite frequent workshops and many community-based activities, it is probably still fair to say that Santa Rosans don't think about inclusivity as often as they should, and tend to downplay the significance of the discrimination that does exist.

CITIZEN INVOLVEMENT

"A cornerstone of sustainability is social equity in the division of limited resources."[81] To be credible, the process of setting priorities must give citizens confidence their views are heard and taken into consideration. In theory the mechanisms to do so are there in almost any American city, including Santa Rosa: voting in elections of city councils, interactions with city boards and commissions, participation in neighborhood associations, and consultation through outreach workshops. In practice, the wealthy and better educated are best able to exploit the system, while the poor and untrained find it difficult to make effective use of it and some are intimidated from even trying.

Dating from the early 1990s, there have been several initiatives to promote greater citizen involvement in Santa Rosa government. A community action task force petered out in the 1990s, and in 2002 a charter revision committee narrowly failed to endorse district elections – that is, election of city council members by separate districts, rather than city-wide, as a means to assure representation of minority ethnic and low- income groups, which are typically found in particular sections of the city.

Efforts on these lines, were unable, however, to achieve significant change. The growth machine that dominated Santa Rosa's government successfully turned aside such pressures, because in the first instance, the City's current system of at-large elections with each candidate running on a city-wide basis favors the machine's candidates, who can exploit mailers, media ads and city-wide advertisements or signs. A district election system on the other hand makes the voter pool small enough in each district so that an individual candidate with few financial resources can rely on handshakes and door-knocks to get his/her message out and achieve name recognition. Also, developers are leery of grassroots single-district candidates because they are more likely to be sympathetic to any neighborhood objections to development projects.

In 2002, following the charter review, Santa Rosa voters by a 3 to 2 margin approved a ballot measure calling for increased citizen participation in government. The pro-developer majority on the City Council implemented the mandate by setting up the Community Advisory Board (CAB) as an alternative to district elections that could ostensibly still serve as a channel for a more direct citizen voice in government. However, the CAB was largely left on the sidelines, given no significant role in the government decision-making process other than to allocate a small fund for promoting neighborhood activities. Moreover, its duties were defined in a way to assure in particular that it would have no meaningful involvement in consideration of development projects.

In any case, the goal became enshrined in Section 10 of the City Charter as "to greatly increase citizen and neighborhood participation and responsibility," and pressure persisted from civic activists to move from the rhetoric to action. In response, the City Administration has used various mechanisms to give citizens more opportunities to make their views known in recent years. Significant examples included the Station Area Specific Plan and the most recent reviews of the General Plan – due in both cases largely to the more open approach espoused by the then-Director of Advance Planning, Wayne Goldberg. Assistant to the City Manager Pat Fruiht has also led outreach efforts of note to gather citizen input on budget and other questions.

How does the city compare with others in this regard? City Manager Jeff Kolin (hired away by Beverly Hills as of January 2010) once observed that Santa Rosa's Administration was in his experience one of the most open to be found among comparable California municipalities. Most progressives, however, would judge the City to still be way short of the mark set by "poster cities" of citizen engagement, such as Portland, Oregon, Seattle, and Boulder, Colorado, or that of less well known Simi Valley, California (population about 120,000), where the entire municipality is divided into neighborhood associations, whose members must be consulted for

---

MAGDALENA RIDLEY
SCRIBE OF ROSELAND –
COMMUNITY ACTIVIST

Magdalena Ridley grew up in Roseland, went off to a top east coast college and returned with a determination to promote community building and inclusivity A gifted writer, her series of op-ed pieces in the Press Democrat pictured a vibrant multicultural Roseland that most people from east Santa Rosa have neither seen nor appreciated.

Ridley has been a passionate advocate for youth and open space. She works as an outreach coordinator at the non-profit Landpaths to manage the wonderfully successful Bayer Farms Neighborhood Park and Garden project and to lead Spanish-language outings that show city kids the great outdoors.

Closer to home in Roseland, she was a founding member of the Roseland Youth Center to sponsor positive after-school recreation programs. And she catalyzed Bloco Rosa, a program to utilize the arts for youth of color to empower them, encourage healthy, active lifestyles; promote leadership for social change and embrace diversity.

A muse for Roseland, Ridley also speaks to the conscience of the Santa Rosa elite, which despite endless meetings and generous contributions to non-profits, has failed to alleviate the sense of "powerless resignation" that all too often pervades the Latino experience in the city.

---

important decisions including all development projects.

The progressive victory in 2008 gave CAB both new members and new impetus. Under Chair Tanya Narath, the CAB took a more pro-active view of its goals and established a more meaningful working relationship with the City Council. As of 2010, however, there seemed no consensus on how or whether to consider major change, such as district elections, establishing an Office of Neighborhood Involvement or other measures to meet the above-mentioned City Charter goal of "greatly increased" citizen participation and responsibility.

DIVERSITY AND DISCRIMINATION

Most Santa Rosans probably believe serious discrimination is a thing of the past. That's a questionable judgment and unfortunately too often serves as an excuse for complacency. A report issued in late 2009 by the local non-profit Listening for a Change (LFAC) observed that the common picture of Sonoma County is that of an idyllic wine country with "community concerns ...airbrushed out." The LFAC report,[82] titled *We Listen*, based its findings on interviews with 77 individuals of varying age and ethnicity, representing minorities, gays and lesbians and physically challenged residents of Sonoma County.

Many, although not all, of the *We Listen* respondents said they had experienced prejudice, cultural ignorance and workplace exclusion. A few found what they considered blatant discrimination or racism, while others described "imaginary lines," and being prejudged, isolated or treated as "strangers." Comments did not suggest Santa Rosa was necessarily less inclusive than similar communities in America or California, but many interviewees were clearly rankled by what they perceived as indifference to real problems.

LFAC recommended nine simple steps that individual citizens could take to help create a more welcoming community. They included, for example, getting personally involved, seeking out new contacts and friends, or volunteering in community work, but public reaction to the report has been muted, and it is hard to see any serious momentum gathering for change. In their private lives, most Santa Rosans appear busy with other matters and slow to appreciate the LFAC findings.

In the face of such experience, a measure of inertia seems to persist, even though innumerable local workshops have concluded more must be done to integrate and better serve minority or disadvantaged segments of the City's population. The City Council has carried forward rhetorical support for diversity in one form or another for years – most recently, in its 2009/10 Goals statement as "Sustain our efforts to make Santa Rosa a more Inclusive Community." For its part, Sonoma County has a formal Commission on the Status of Women and one on Human

Rights, but both are widely regarded as ineffective, and neither can point to any substantial recent record of action.

The lurking presence of extreme ethnic bias was graphically illustrated in 2008/9 by the persistence of hateful and ignorant comments posted on Press Democrat website news stories. Any crime report involving a Hispanic surname provoked a string of anti-immigrant, anti-Latino insults, while articles about criminal acts by persons with common European surnames evoked few comments, and virtually none with ethnic overtones. In February 2010, the Press Democrat stopped allowing readers to post comments on website news stories, and an editor wrote a tepid explanation about changing the system because of "inappropriate" and sometimes "offensive" remarks – leaving the underlying racism issues under the rug.[83] Ironically, the city's School Board at about the same time rejected parent objections to use in high schools of *Tortilla Curtain*, a contemporary novel with language very similar to the real-life online comments, although spiced with obscenities.

But the Santa Rosa School Board is not yet representative of the community it serves. In October 2008, official figures showed enrollment at 52.5% Latino students in elementary schools and near 31% in high schools, while the seven-member board had only one Latino Member, Laura Gonzalez. In February 2010, the Board's paternalistic establishment streak showed itself when the majority voted against issuing Certificates of Course Completion to High school seniors who had met all graduation requirements except for passing the state-mandated exit exam. Four white members in effect substituted their judgment for that of Latino parents who testified the Certificates would greatly help motivate English learning children in their community to stay in school until graduation day despite their test-taking difficulties.

INCLUSIVITY AND BUILDING COMMUNITY

With respect to racial discrimination, the situation in general is much better in Santa Rosa today than it was as recently as the 1980s, when educated African-Americans were advised they would do better to seek employment "further south" or maybe "in Vallejo." Things have changed since then, due to efforts over many years by people like Gilbert Gray, who formed the County's NAACP Chapter, and James and Carole Ellis Coffee, who came here in 1963, she as a teacher and he as Pastor of Community Baptist Church. Other path-finders in racial equality and social justice movements included George Ortiz, Essie Parish, Alicia Sanchez, Song Wong Bourbeau, all complemented and followed by a host of social justice advocates in faith-based organizations and non-profits – far too many to mention here.

In response to the public will expressed in the 2002 ballot measure, the City Council also amended the City Charter to promote diversity as well as citizen participation. Section 11 provides that the Council shall "undertake all reasonable methods to ensure that its appointments to boards, commissions and committees reflect Santa Rosa's diversity, including geographic and ethnic diversity." That was an important step and it has had a positive effect, even though it continued the city's top-down approach as opposed to more "organic" or grassroots measures.

Barriers have fallen for election to the City Council. A powerful symbolic blow was struck for inclusivity in 2004 when Lee Pierce won election as the first person of color to sit on the City Council. In 2008, Ernesto Olivares became the first Latino to do so. In both cases, however, it must be noted that for their successful runs, they were chosen as candidates not by community grassroots organizations, but by a political machine with the white developer establishment at the controls. This is not a reflection on either of the individuals, but rather on the system as it exists. Pierce, to his great credit as described in the early chapters of this book, maintained his personal independence and proved more responsive to citizens at large than to the developer interests that financed his winning campaign in 2004.

For their part, Latinos have been slowly mobilizing themselves, led by such personalities as Caroline Bañuelos, Efren Carrillo, Oscar Chavez, Rene Meza, Juan Nieto, Jaime Peñaherrera, Patricia Robles-Mitten, David Rosas, Miguel Ruelas, Wanda Tapia, Francisco H. Vázquez. Perhaps the single most influential channel of interaction with the larger political-economic community has been the Hispanic Chamber of Commerce of Sonoma County, which was organized in 1988 and as of 2010 has nearly 400 members.[84] The Chamber does not have an overtly political role, but it does include the political in its broad goals statement: "Through membership, our voices can be heard in the political, social, economic, and educational arenas." And a relatively new Latino Democratic Club has been organized under the aegis of the Sonoma County Democratic Central Committee.

In recent years, a number of active community-based social programs and organizations have also registered important gains. The Sonoma County Community Action Partnership (CAP) has long had one of the larger and most successful programs, working with low-income families to help them achieve economic stability, build community and advocate for social justice. Under its dynamic leader, Oscar Chavez, CAP has been able to expand its funding and intensify programming for youth and ESL. HEAL (Healthy Eating, Active Living), sponsored by Sonoma County with strong support from Kaiser Permanente and other businesses, has a primary focus on healthy food and physical activity, but its community building arm has also trained numerous Latinos how to advocate and address issues with local government.

Like CAP and HEAL, a range of activities from churches to the La Voz newspaper to the City's Neighborhood Revitalization Program and the Mayor's Task Force on Gang Prevention are not specifically organized to promote inclusivity, but that is inevitably an important impact of nearly all such organizations. Increasing awareness of the benefits from better integration has helped steer resources their way. More and more Latino leaders are also stepping forward to help build community – as did Rene Meza, who played the pivotal role in transforming Santa Rosa's Cinco de Mayo festival from a sometimes rowdy street mixer to an outstanding cultural event, with participation by people of all ages from across the City and County.

The recent history of programs to teach adults English as a Second Language (ESL) illustrates both the successes and shortfalls of community effort. Good language skills are obviously essential for participation in the broader community and, moreover, the Sonoma County Innovation Council identified ESL as essential to build the workforce sorely needed for local industry and business. The County Library has offered ESL classes, but results have been limited owing to funding limitations and lack of childcare facilities. Santa Rosa School District adult programs were cut to nothing in 2009, when state-wide education budgets were slashed to rock-bottom levels. And the Santa Rosa Chamber of Commerce also found it necessary because of the recession to cut back funding for its programs to promote English learning. CAP has stepped up to fill some of the gap with new ESL programs for 2010 following on its acquisition of space in the Lewis Adult School left empty by the School District cuts, but it can only do so much with what it has.

On the voter front, a group of Latino leaders met in 2007 to discuss ways to promote the visibility and representation of their community in local politics. Along with the Community Foundation Sonoma County and the Hutchins Institute for Public Policy Studies and Community Action at Sonoma State University, they convened a non-partisan Coalition for Latino Civic Engagement (CLACE). The broader group included numerous leading lights from across the political spectrum, among others: Senator Pat Wiggins, the League of Women Voters, Herb Williams, and SEIU. CLACE set itself ambitious goals to increase Latino voter participation and support candidates that could effectively represent Latino interests – but its impact appeared limited at best with sporadic door-knocking by high school students leading up to the 2008 elections and a website that as of 2010 reads the same as it apparently did on late 2007. Perhaps it will spring into action for the 2010 elections.

In sum, there is a lot going on in Santa Rosa, but overall progress on inclusivity is slower than it should be – to the detriment of not only the minority groups, but also the community as a whole.

HERITAGE PRESERVATION

In its way, one of the most telling comments on Santa Rosa's insularity has been the failure to recognize non-European heritage in historic preservation. The Carrillo Adobe, built in 1837, is unquestionably one of the most important historic sites in the State. It was the home of Maria Lopez de Carrillo, the mother-in-law of General Vallejo and recipient in 1841 of a 4,500 acre land grant – the Cabeza de Santa Rosa Rancho – that, so to speak, put Santa Rosa, California on the map to stay.

The adobe itself might well have been saved. Much of the building remained in good condition until the 1940s, when parts of the roof and walls collapsed. Then, some two-thirds of what was still there in the 1960s subsequently melted away as a consequence of continuing neglect. Nonetheless, even today, the few bricks left are still evocative enough to inspire dreams of a fine public park with a wonderfully educational exhibit of Santa Rosa's Mexican heritage...and of the Pomo Indians, who had a village or possibly a sacred burial ground on the site before that.

Despite past talk and promises, as of 2010, any museum cum park for the Adobe seems yet far distant in the future. Only a few archeological researchers and preservationists have given more than lip service to the memorial park idea – they continue to wait for the long-delayed improvements and transfer of the site to the City from developers planning an apartment complex surrounding what's left of the Adobe.

The City's Chinese heritage has fared no better. Not even a few bricks are left of Santa Rosa's Chinatown, erased from its location east of Courthouse Square over the years by the city's white leaders, in part perhaps for economic reasons, but mostly it seems because such a visible Chinese presence was not wanted so near the town's center. By the 1950s only one Chinese restaurant, the Jam Kee, remained, but it too is long gone and with it the final physical trace of downtown's Chinese residents, who despite gross mistreatment and patent discrimination, played an important role in Santa Rosa from the mid-nineteenth century onward.[85]

When Santa Rosa leaders finally did take notice of historic preservation, they focused almost exclusively on the Europeans who symbolized the quintessentially American transformation of the area. In 1964, Luther Burbank's Home and Gardens became a national Historic Landmark. Interest picked up in the 1970s, and in 1979, Railroad Square was added to the National Register of Historic Places. It wasn't until 1988, however, that the Santa Rosa City Council passed a preservation ordinance and established the Cultural Heritage Board (CHB) to foster protection of the city's Historic Districts. Still, as late as 2004, pro-developer former Mayor and Council Member Mike Martini remarked, "Santa Rosa needs room to grow," and promptly voted with the majority to deny protection for a well kept block of turn-of- the-century Victorian cottages on Orchard Street.

The Sonoma County Historical Society has maintained active programs to record and celebrate the area's past, including a strong effort to promote interest in saving the Carrillo Adobe. A more city-oriented preservation advocacy group, SRPAST (Santa Rosa Preservation Advocacy Support Taskforce), was founded in 2004 by Susan Clark,

Dan Flock, Denise Hill and others in large part to counter the potential encroachment on historic districts by high-rise development proposed at the time.

Recognition of historical contributions and preservation of heritage is important for inclusivity. The sprinkling of Hispanic street names or passing references to Chinese, Japanese and African-American contributions does little to make minority groups feel a part of the city's fabric, especially when compared to the attention given to the many European sites and surnames. Some community leaders – Nancy Wang of the Redwood Empire Chinese Association is one exemplary advocate – have sought to close the gap, but progress has been slow.

SOCIAL, EDUCATIONAL AND RECREATIONAL SERVICES

Maintaining adequate social and educational services is key to any city's overall health and sustainability. In Santa Rosa, the governmental part of the job falls to three separate but interrelated jurisdictions: the City, the County and the Santa Rosa School District. The County has a leading role in health and human services, while the City is in the forefront for recreational programs, including those targeted for seniors and at-risk youth within City limits, although private organizations carry a tremendous part of the load in all these areas. The City owns the 120-bed Samuel L. Jones homeless shelter, which is operated by Catholic Charities with the help also of the County and Community Foundation.

For both the young and old, the City has well-developed recreation amenities, most notably perhaps the Senior Center, the Ridgway and Finley swimming pools, and Howarth Park with its boating and children's playground. These very popular programs generally survived through the 2009/10 budget year with increases in fees or diminished levels of service, but the City's ongoing fiscal woes will force more cutbacks. Santa Rosa is ranked sixth in the nation among cities for population over 85 years of age and for the needy among them, the non-profit Council on Aging can be literally a life saver. In 2009, the Council helped nearly one third of the county's 70,000 over-60 population with assistance ranging from meals-on-wheels to legal and financial services to individual care and case management.

For youth, Santa Rosa has a tradition of fine schools and associated activities. Although the city's School District is funded and managed separately from the City Administration, there is close cooperation between the two entities, including for example a Safe School's program with the participation of the Santa Rosa Police Department. The School District, County and City also work together on a variety of activities for youth, not least with reference to the health programs and those for at-risk young people from low-income families or areas threatened by gang influence. The County administers the Public Library along with its literacy and language outreach, that now includes special attention to children and to those weak in English, especially of course newly immigrant Latinos

Private sector organizations are the mainstay providers of social services to the needy around the clock. In addition to the Council on Aging, major contributors include the Community Action Partnership (also mentioned earlier), Southwest Community Health Center, DeMeo CHOP'S Teen Center, Catholic Charities, Committee on the Shelterless (COTS), the YWCA, the Living Room day center for homeless women and their children, Redwood Empire Food Bank, Social Advocates for Youth (SAY), Big Brothers/Big Sisters and a host of others too numerous to mention here. Along with government agencies, the local Community Foundation of Sonoma County has become a major provider of funds and greatly increased its endowment over the last decade. Other sources include the United Way of Sonoma, Mendocino and Lake Counties, along with hundreds of individual and business donors,

AFFORDABLE HOUSING

Affordable housing has been a major problem throughout the State and is something of a special case for public policy of city governments like Santa Rosa. Quotas or targets are set by the regional authority – ABAG – and a city's failure to make good faith efforts to meet the specified goals can jeopardize much needed grant support from State or Federal authorities. State law also mandates that 20% of redevelopment agency funds must be devoted to affordable housing. And everybody agrees that affordable housing is vital for both the economy and a healthy society with diverse age groups and a range of workforce skills.

In Santa Rosa, housing became more and more unaffordable as the building boom gathered steam in the early 2000s. By mid-2006 only 23% of Sonoma County first-time homebuyers were able to afford the then medium-priced home costing around $550,000. About 60% of renters that year were spending more than 30% of their income on housing and over 25% were severely burdened by rentals taking more than 50% of their income. In August 2005 the median home price peaked at $619,000, but plummeted with the Great Recession and hit less than half that number at $305,000 in February 2009. By December 2009, the median was back to $389,000 and rising.[86] If the recession has had any silver lining in Sonoma County, it would be the increase in housing affordability. As of March 2009, around the low point for the median home price, 63% of county households could aspire to buy a home,[87] although financing remained difficult to get.

In any case, for the period 2007-2014, ABAG has developed a Regional Housing Needs Assessment (RHNA – pronounced "ree-na" by housing experts). It provides the framework to set goals for the City based on projections of household size, employment and population, including the ABAG calculation that an additional 70,000 residents will come into the city by 2035. RHNA targets are set by income categories. For example, "moderate" means affordable to a family of four earning between 80% and 120% of the county area's median income of something over $80,000 in 2009 for that category. Low Income affordability refers to income between 50% and 80%; Very Low to between 30% and 50%; and the recently added category of Extremely Low refers to income less than 30%.

The revision of the General Plan Housing Element in 2009 generated heated discussion over how to approach the RHNA targets. Implementation of housing policy is determined not by the General Plan itself, but by an ordinance which spells out the Housing Allocation Plan (HAP). As indicated above in Chapter 9, the Station Area Specific Plan (SASP) changed long-standing guidelines in ways that would require developers to put more affordable units on site in the same complex higher-priced housing, and would also promote a more balance dispersion of affordable homes across the city. The SASP applied only to the area around Railroad Square, and developers in late 2009 mounted vigorous efforts to prevent its approach from being applied to the entire city by the HAP, which was to be revised in 2010 to implement the revised General Plan.

A carefully balanced citizens' committee was selected in late 2009 by the Mayor to consider HAP revisions. The split soon became obvious as developers with support from the Chamber of Commerce maintained that the existing system should not be radically changed, since it "wasn't broke." Such a position was defensible in their eyes because by ABAG count, Santa Rosa produced the third highest total of affordable units among all cities in the Bay Area. Progressives on the HAP Committee were not so impressed by the total volume figures, given that Santa Rosa is the fifth largest city in the area, meaning that proportionately, it exceeded only Oakland and Fremont in volume of production. More relevant for the progressives was performance against targets by category – Santa Rosa only met 88% of its overall target and, more to the point, the city achieved only 38% of its target for very low income units. A number of other cities did much better on these counts, with Petaluma for example, having produced over 100% in all three categories and 126% of its total.

As of early 2010, the HAP committee remained at loggerheads. There was some give from the developer side on dispersion and methodology and some from the progressives on flexibility of implementation. If the gap cannot be overcome, the matter will go back to the City Council, where something close to the SASP model would likely prevail, given that that approach for the HAP had earlier been approved by the Planning Commission.

POLITICS AND PERCEPTIONS

Can we measure social sustainability in Santa Rosa? A report card on the topics discussed above would probably give the city pretty good marks compared to other cities of its size in America. The beneficial location, relative wealth, liberal views and civic traditions have all helped mobilize resources for social programs. As mentioned in Chapter 8 above, a national survey measuring health and well-being for 2009 found Sonoma County tops in California and fifth best in the country on its index, which takes into account life evaluation, emotional health, physical health, healthful behavior, work environment, and basic access to necessities.[88]

There is still a political divide, however, when it comes to what Santa Rosa can or should be doing for inclusivity, citizen engagement and affordable housing. The 2002 Charter Review Commission and its aftermath did not resolve the issues of what in progressive eyes is the city's lagging performance on knocking down social barriers and getting more residents involved more directly in their own governance. As for the clash over affordable housing, the issue is focused on rather narrow policy goals and will probably move to Council decision in 2010.

Budget crunches for at least the next few years will limit City Hall's options to become more pro-active on the inclusivity and citizen engagement fronts. It will be difficult, for example, to fund the kind of city offices to support neighborhood involvement that other cities have built into their municipal organizations. Similarly, investment of funds and personnel time for activities like conferences, studies or workshops to promote inclusivity may be resisted as government departments scramble to fulfill their existing missions.

Much could be accomplished by cost-free changes in attitude and policy. There have been steps in this direction, for example Mayor Gorin's outreach to community leaders and the more open approach taken by the City's Boards and Commissions. Overall, however, progressives have yet to pull together a plan or articulate a program that could give more priority to social sustainability and the subset of issues treated in this chapter.

The concluding chapter of this book follows to pull together the dangling threads and ask what comes next in city politics…and suggest why Santa Rosans should care.

CHAPTER 13

GOVERNMENT MATTERS – DEMOCRATIZING SANTA ROSA

Does it make a difference who sits on the City Council in Santa Rosa for the next few years? You bet – wrenching revolution is unlikely, but inspired leadership could reshape the city's vision of itself, pursue sustainability across the board, and engage more citizens in the business of governing.

Important Council decisions loom ahead for Santa Rosa on the issues reviewed in the preceding three chapters. Chief among them are how to achieve environmental sustainability, cope with demographic change, and shape the development of the city's center. The possibility of decisive city-changing action is there, even though Councils will continue to be faced with national economic uncertainties, ongoing City budget shortfalls, regulation imposed from above, tough local politicking and at times, bureaucratic inertia.

Vigorous competition will endure for control of the City Council, pitting the relatively small but wealthy and influential coalition of land development interests against grassroots organizations. The stakes are high and voter perceptions may be difficult to discern.

The first test for the staying power of Santa Rosa's progressive majority will come in 2010, but every election year thereafter could swing the pendulum one way or the other. This concluding chapter looks at how election results will likely affect the major policy decisions that lie ahead, and how political maneuvering seeks to frame the agenda in the contest for public support at the ballot box.

PROGRESSIVES – MAKING A DIFFERENCE, BUT HOW BIG?

The first progressive majority on the City Council brought new inclusivity and openness to Santa Rosa government. Mayor Gorin, for example, continued to go to all the business events such as Chamber of Commerce breakfasts, but unlike her predecessors, she also started periodic meetings with a range of community leaders from neighborhood, social and environmental groups and organizations. Then too, Council influence was evident in the selection of a new Police Chief, chosen in large measure because of his declared commitment to improved "community-based" policing – a stark contrast to his two authoritarian predecessors, who seemed stiff and unapproachable to many citizens.

In a similar vein, the newly-appointed city board and commission members from their first days on the job gave higher priority to engaging the community and listening to neighborhood voices. The Planning Commission, which for years was perceived to have relatively little interest in the input of "ordinary folk," showed itself under its new Chairperson, Vicki Duggan, more willing to give time to hear neighborhood views – and indeed to assure opportunity for input from all quarters, as when it extended General Plan hearings for weeks in response to requests from some business representatives who felt left out of the early review stages. The Design Review Board, under former City Planner, Ken MacNab, similarly made a particular point of getting neighborhood input – MacNab had been widely praised for his wide-ranging community consultations when he led development of the Station Area Plan while working in the City's Advanced Panning office.

A policy shift to stress environmental concerns also came into play soon after the elections of November 2008. As noted previously, the Council gave early direction to revise the standards upward in the Green Building Ordinance, and the Mayor with majority backing appointed a progressive member and alternative transportation advocate, Gary Wysocky, to replace his pro-developer colleague, John Sawyer, on the important Sonoma County Transportation Authority (SCTA). Over the early months also, the Council majority signaled deep misgivings on environmental grounds about two major development projects – a Lowe's big box store application and a residential complex in Fountaingrove. Fearing lawsuits, the Council approved the EIRs submitted for the projects, but both failed to gain final approvals in the subsequent phases of their applications.

Another distinguishing feature of the progressive Council majority has been its willingness to challenge development policies that have not been seriously reviewed since they were formed in the quite different circumstance of the 1990s. The most notable example was its questioning of a proposal to use over $5 million of City funds for a large new parking garage to be built in connection with a "boutique hotel" project downtown. Council Members in the pro-developer minority argued for moving ahead even though the garage would be underutilized for years, and they helped stir up a minor political firestorm over the issue. In the end, however, the garage died from lack of adequate financing before the Council took any definitive action. Some insistently blamed the progressive majority for the project's demise, but the hotel cum garage project was an iffy investment from the start, and no one should have been surprised when it fell victim to the same kind of financing problems that killed the previous White House site proposal despite enthusiastic support from strongly pro-developer Councils.

Going into its second year the Council's agenda was dominated by the need to deal with the unrelenting budget crunch. Its main options – deep cuts or new taxes – were unattractive to say the least. The Council did, however, forge ahead on drafting of ordinances on campaign finances and lobbyist registration to lay down markers in favor of clean government. The Mayor also continued to press for establishment of a Sustainability Taskforce – at her request, City departments started working in 2009 to set up an overarching system for City Hall coordination of "green" issues, but high-level administrators appeared uneasy with the idea of Council Member participation in such an animal.

Still, there has not been much progress on inclusivity. District elections have proven "too hot to handle" for the time being. With no apparent upswell of public opinion, key leaders are unwilling to step out in front and the Council has shown no interest. This could change radically when the next Charter Review gets underway – it is mandated to take place by 2012 and the process would likely start in 2011, which is to say after elections in 2010. Census figures from 2010 will be very important in this regard.

As for development policy and urban planning, going into 2010 elections, the picture is mixed despite the principled positions the Council majority took in 2009, with its relatively strong defense of local business and insistence on environmental protections. The idea, for example, that the Station Area Plan should be modified to accommodate the desires of a few property owners in the Maxwell Court area (Chapter 9 above) smacked of buckling to political pressures. The proposal to annex a large parcel for development in southeast also threatened to detract from the focus on transit-oriented development around the SMART stations.

SO WHAT WOULD *REALLY* CHANGE?

Guessing what any City Council will do is risky, even foolhardy. The idea here, however, is not so much to predict specific actions, as it is to sort out the main areas of Council activity, identify points of contention, and ask how the two factions are likely to act when faced with decisions. Over the years, an extensive record of debate and Council voting has been compiled. Even a cursory survey goes far to lay out marked differences of views between the two sides on many key issues, and to show as well significant areas of agreement. Much of course can depend on personalities and even more may hinge on external factors beyond Council control, and with those caveats, historical review of recent years offers a projection something like the following of future Council deliberations:

Environmental sustainability: On this buzz-word topic, future Council agendas will include natural resource protection, energy efficiency, greenhouse gas reductions, habitat conservation and open space preservation. Both sides will support initiatives such as the SMART train, promotion of green enterprises, and environmentally pro-active City operations like hybrid buses, although seriously reducing overall Vehicle Miles Traveled (VMT) by city residents will be a difficult proposition for years to come. In any case, progressives will apply considerably higher standards for new development as they seek project by project to minimize adverse environmental impacts, promote alternative transportation and reduce GHG emissions. Pro-developer council members will be prone to cut environmental corners to help development projects "pencil out."

Diversity: This has become a code word meaning greater integration of our growing Latino community. No one is against such inclusivity, but the establishment associated with the growth machine favors a top-down approach that keeps decision-making – and hence social program priorities – in the hands of the city's elite. This was demonstrated clearly by the City Council's earlier determined opposition to District Elections and unwillingness to give a neighborhood development review function to the Community Advisory Board. Progressives, although divided on whether to proceed with District Elections, will be willing to explore that option and other ways to give a stronger voice to Latinos and other minorities.

Vibrant downtown: Santa Rosa's downtown may have lost a measure of "vibrancy" over the years as business activity flowed away to suburban shopping and office centers, but it has avoided outright decay, thanks to efforts that have enlivened Railroad Square and 4th Street along with the substantial level of office occupancy. Pro-developer Council majorities subsidized local developer Larry Wasem's Roxy Stadium Theater with parking in the public garage, and later on sought to attract other large-scale building projects such as 10 to 14 story mixed-use buildings and another large City parking garage – by all indications this expansive vision will continue to drive their decisions. Progressives are skeptical that traditional auto-dependent projects will in fact bring in a sustainable level of further development, and they will support alternative approaches, notably SMART station area projects in line with goals of transit oriented developments and reduction of Greenhouse Gases. In early 2010, a new proposal for the vacant AT&T building drew considerable praise for its design and prospective use by the Sonoma County Museum, but reaction to the possibility of a new large County Court House on the site of the central Post Office was greeted with relatively little enthusiasm.

Positive business climate: Both major factions agree that the City should promote its existing businesses and work to attract new ones. Progressives tend to emphasize building on the local base while positioning the City as a Mecca for innovation and "green" industry – Mayor Gorin and the 2009 Council also fully supported the City's downtown business promotion programs. Council members elected with support from the growth machine will be more willing than progressives to walk back environmental and design regulations, although both factions seem willing to consider temporary measures to mitigate the drag of the slow economic recovery following the "Great Recession." The local business community has closely followed the lead of major developers, but that could change as interests become more divergent in the 21st century.

Stable city budget: Creating a stronger revenue base for the city budget is high on everyone's list. Some remain firmly persuaded that big box stores and new shopping centers will increase tax revenues, but as the Lowe's case showed in 2009, it is hard, perhaps impossible, to demonstrate there would be any net gain to the General Fund given Santa Rosa's generally saturated market and highly stressed infrastructure, such as congested roads. Instead of more big boxes, many progressives look to building on existing enterprises, including measures such as strengthening tourism and emphasizing local sources (e.g., GoLocal) for goods and services. In the end, however, stable budget financing will depend heavily on factors beyond the City's control, in particular the health of the national economy and the distant prospect of reform at the state level.

Growth and development: Harvey Molotch, reflecting on his years of research about urban politics, observed, "the trick is to distinguish positive change from regressive change."[89] For Molotch, projects make local sense only if they pay for themselves over the long run, they provide good jobs, they improve distributive justice and they are environmentally benign. Similar ideas are woven through the approach of Santa Rosa progressives, while the pro-developer side hews to an "all growth is good" mantra, modified to go green where practicable. The nature of development policy will probably continue as the most significant factional divide.

2010, 2012, AND BEYOND

Pro-developer strategists began early to frame the agenda for 2010 elections in ways favorable to their candidates. Playing off recession-induced economic worries, they have sought to paint Council progressives as "anti-business," studiously avoiding praise for the Council majority when it helped Railroad Square developers or when it defended local businesses threatened by the Lowe's big-box application. The second major attack line emerging from the pro-developer machine's economic interests is directed against labor unions, trying to brand them as a "special interest" responsible for higher costs to home-buyers and taxpayers. A third line being honed in early 2010 for the pro-developer City Council campaign is that environmental regulations impede profitable development – their code word is "balance," used in effect to accuse environmentalists of going too far.

Progressives will continue to push their environmental, quality of life and social justice agendas. Their case rests on the newly-urgent need to protect and conserve the area's natural resources, to work for a more just and integrated society, and to channel development into more beneficial directions. They will try to build on their record of supporting local business and local development projects that measure up on environmental grounds. Their insight is sustainability over short-term economic gain.

In 2010, three seats will be open on the City Council. With a year to go before elections in November 2010, incumbent progressives Gorin and Jacobi are expected to run again. The third seat is that of pro-developer Council Member Bender, who was intending to retire in 2008, but stayed on to run for and win the two year term that remained after the untimely demise of her close colleague, then-Mayor Bob Blanchard.

The math is simple. If incumbents Gorin and Jacobi retain their seats, the progressive side will hold its majority for two more years. If Bender retires and a progressive is able to capture the vacancy, the majority will be strengthened. For its part, the pro-developer machine will of course be working hard to keep Bender's seat and defeat one of the two progressive incumbents to regain its majority position. In 2012, four seats will again be open, and control of the Council may well hinge on a shift of only one seat.

The patterns of 2008 electioneering seem likely to repeat for the next few cycles. The $45,000 limit on campaign spending by any one candidate will become effective for the first time in 2010, but candidates in 2008 were already making do with less as the economic downturn reduced campaign contributions across the board. The tightly organized growth machine economized effectively with the unified slate approach described in Chapter 3. Progressives have continued to work as cooperating independent candidates, and some have resisted a slate approach on principle, although the new economics may push them closer together as election day approaches.

POLITICS AND DEMOCRACY IN SANTA ROSA

At the core for years to come, Santa Rosa politicking will revolve around the familiar land development issues. The dynamics outlined in the early chapters of this book continue to operate, as the wealth tied up in exploitation of land values repositions itself for the changed circumstances of coming years. The Titanic-sized crash of Clem Carinalli's empire and the slew of smaller bankruptcies are bound to bring a major shake-out, but a great deal of money still rides on development of the open acres remaining within the Urban Growth Boundary.

Politics being politics, the machine will fuzz the core issue of undue developer influence and exploit its organizational advantage through artful campaign materials, effective use of polls, and emphasis on name recognition, enhanced by extensive media advertising, signs and mailer floods. Unless the Press Democrat management changes unexpectedly, the growth machine will be able to rely on the city's only daily for continued invaluable support.

Come elections, the burden will be on progressives to show they are the better team. In this regard, despite obvious differences of circumstance, the lessons of Santa Cruz may well apply – that city is one of the relatively few in America where progressives defeated an embedded growth machine and subsequently held on to City Council majorities year in, year out. Academics on the scene who made a case study,[90] drew two main conclusions for progressives elsewhere: first, activists must be "highly committed" and "find ways to work together to create the widest possible coalition...(but not) lose their focus and zeal;" and second, activists must "develop the patience and trust to make their presence felt in the electoral arena." Tall orders!

Can progressives successfully attract voters in 2010 and beyond? The liberal lean of Santa Rosa voters should favor progressive ideas hands down, but in American elections, as all political junkies know, the framing of the issue can be more important than the merits of the issue itself. The pro-developer machine will work hard to persuade citizens that expansive growth is still the path to prosperity. Progressives have to articulate the superior case – that times have changed, and Santa Rosa must now measure its governmental policies against the yardsticks of sustainability for its well-being.

Potentially, however, the more important dynamic of Santa Rosa politics is the willingness of citizens to seek more direct influence on their city's governance. In Santa Rosa over the last two decades, progressive community groupings surged on three occasions to push back against the growth machine:

- in the early 1990s when they achieved a Growth Management Ordinance and the Urban Growth Boundary;

- around the turn of the millennium when they promoted New Urbanist planning and unsuccessfully sought district elections; and

- in the late 2000s when they opposed undue developer influence to gain their first-ever Council majority.

From that perspective, a continued groundswell of grassroots support for citizen engagement, inclusivity, and environmental protections could end growth machine dominance and transform Santa Rosa into a city closer to the cutting edge of sustainability for the 21st century.

Acknowledgments

I am deeply indebted to many engaged citizens who shared their information and insights with me. I also admire and appreciate the many activists – whether they identify with the progressive coalition, the growth machine or neither – who have worked for a variety of selfless causes intended to improve quality of life in our community, promote inclusivity, and sustain the environment.

I am particularly grateful to Maria Halyna Lewytzkyj who read a final draft text with a sound editorial and proofing eye. Thank you also to those who granted me thought-provoking interviews in the early days as I was just forming the ideas for this book: Jenny Bard, Christine Culver, Susan Gorin, Mike Harmon, David McCuan, Lee Pierce, and Magdalena Ridley, among others. Many City employees up and down the line also gave invaluable assistance in response to my requests for information and documentation.

Finally, I have to give appreciative nods to three first-rate Press Democrat writers for their major contributions to my source materials: Mike McCoy for his exceptional coverage of Santa Rosa political happenings; to Chris Coursey for his insightful columns on local politics and their social consequences; and to Gaye LeBaron for her columns filling in the historical background with skill and flair.

I hope this book accurately portrays both the events described and the opinions imputed to others – to the extent that it does not, the blame is mine alone.

Endnotes

1. Editorial staff, "SR City Council," *The Press Democrat,* October 15, 2000

2. Mike McCoy, "Developer again top council campaign donor," *The Press Democrat,* October 28, 2006

3. See http://www.marshavasdupre.com/Council2002/The%20 real%20story.htm

4. Sonoma County Statement of Votes, Consolidated General Election, November 7, 2006 from http://www.sonoma-county. org/RegVoter/elections/2006.htm The County Registrar of Voters reports votes for candidates as a percentage of all votes cast for the position of Council Member. Since there were three open seats in 2006, the number of such votes cast could be up to three on each ballot. Gorin polled 24,263 votes from a total of 54,234 individual ballots cast, which is to say 44.7% of those who voted gave her the nod. The Registrar reported Gorin as winning 18.9% of the total vote, with the total derived by counting as three votes all those ballots marked for three different candidates, two votes for all ballots marked with two entries, etc.

5. Paul Payne, "SR Council drops voluntary spending caps," *The Press Democrat,* December 20, 2006

6. Chris Coursey, "Putting the 97-lb Weakling in His Place," *The Press Democrat,* December 29, 2006

7. Chris Coursey, "3-3 council has 50-50 chance of fractiousness," *The Press Democrat,* July 2, 2007

8. Press Democrat, "SANTA ROSA CITY COUNCIL CAMPAIGN FUND RAISING," *The Press Democrat,* February 6, 2009

9. Gaye LeBaron, "Reality sets in: Santa Rosa is no longer a sleepy farm town," *The Press Democrat,* March 4, 2007

10. This chapter draws heavily from the literature on urban growth coalition theory, in particular the writings of Harvey Molotch, John Logan, Clarence Stone and G. William Domhoff. In addition to the articles of those authors, the primary books consulted included the classic John R Logan and Harvey L. Molotch (1987). *Urban Fortunes: The Political Economy of Place.* Berkeley: University of California Press, and Andrew. E.g. Jonas and David Wilson (editors) (1999). *The Urban Growth Machine: Critical Perspectives Two Decades Later.* State University of New York Press.

11. Logan and Molotch (1987)

12. G. William Domhoff (2005). "Power at the Local Level: Growth Coalition theory," from the author's website, http:// sociology.ucsc.edu/whorulesamerica/power/local.html

13. Domhoff (2005)

14. Logan and Molotch (1987)

15. Clarence N. Stone (1989), *Regime Politics: Governing Atlanta 1949-1988,* University Press of Kansas

16. Edwin Stennett (2002), *In Growth We Trust: Sprawl, Smart Growth, and Rapid Population Growth,* Gaithersburg, Md., Growth Education Movement, Inc., 2002

17. Jay Hancock. "Officials Base Subsidies On Flawed Model," *The Baltimore Sun*, October 12, 1999, quoting Timothy Bartik of the Upjohn Institute for Employment research

18. Paul D. Gottlieb (2002). "Growth Without Growth," Brookings Institution, Washington, D.C.

19. Gaye LeBaron and Joann Mitchell (1993) *Santa Rosa, A 20th Century Town,* Santa Rosa, Historia Ltd.LeBaron

20. Lebaron and Mitchell (1993) pg 331

21. Tom Chorneau, "Diversity for SR Council doubtful," *The Press Democrat,* October 27, 1996

22. Chris Coursey, "Putting the 97-pound Weakling in his Place," *The Press Democrat,* December 29,2006

23. Tom Chorneau, "SR Mayor to Head Business Group," *The Press Democrat,* August 11, 2002

24. See the SCA website: www.sonomacounty alliance.com

25. State of California, Fair Political Practices Commission, *Bulletin,* Vol. 24., No. 1, February 1998

26. Mike McCoy, "Power Player," *The Press Democrat,* March 24, 2005

27. Mike McCoy, "Polls help Williams take the pulse of voters," *The Press Democrat,* April 17, 2005

28. Mike McCoy, "Power Player," *The Press Democrat,* March 24, 2005

29. David Rosas, "Political, personal lessons from SR council race loss," *The Press Democrat,* November 9, 2008

30. personal conversation with the author

31. Bleys Rose, "Independent groups spent big in supe races," *The Press Democrat,* February 6, 2009

32. see Domhoff (2005) "Power at the Local Level"

33. see John R. Logan and Harvey L. Molotch (2007), *Urban Fortunes: the Political Economy of Place,* 20th Anniversary Edition, Berkeley, University of California Press

34. LeBaron and Mitchell (1993)

35. See SCCA website: *www.conservationaction.org/*

36. Chris Coursey, "Council Votes to Keep Status Quo," *The Press Democrat,* July 31, 2002

37. see Paul Payne, "Fighting for Affordable Housing," *The Press Democrat,* May 11, 2003.

38. Mary Fricker, "Labor's Challenge in a New Century," *The Press Democrat,* March 8, 2004

39. Mike McCoy, "City Council Campaign Spending Records Fall," *The Press Democrat*, February 2, 2001

40. Nathan Halverson, "Happiest Place in California," *The Press Democrat*, February 16, 2010

41. Thomas Friedman, "Welcome to the 'Great Disruption." *New York Times*, March 9, 2009

42. Mike McCoy, "City, county officials quizzed in quest for Santa Rosa's identity," *The Press Democrat*, February 6, 2007

43. Bob Norberg, "SR" A City in Search of an Identity," *The Press Democrat*, May 24, 2007

44. This section draws heavily from LeBaron and Mitchell (1993), along with Ms. LeBaron's many excellent retrospective articles from the Press Democrat.

45. LeBaron and Mitchell (1993) p131

46. Lebaron and Mitchell (1993) p 335

47. http://ci.santa-rosa.ca.us/doclib/Documents/EDH_History_and_accomplishments.pdf

48. http://www.seismo-watch.com/EQSERVICES/NotableEQ/Oct/1001.SantaRosa.html

49. See the EIR for Lowe's, available from the Santa Rosa Community Development Department and posted (accessed January 4, 2010) on the City website at http://ci.santa-rosa.ca.us/departments/communitydev/development/Pages/CD_EIR_Lowes.aspx

50. Magdalena Ridley, "Roseland redevelopment should not be for the rich," *The Press Democrat*, March 18, 2007

51. Bleys W. Rose, "Going Negative," *The Press Democrat*, October 28, 2008

52. from the Sonoma County website, accessed June 8, 2009: http://www.sonoma-county.org/cao/citizens_guide/sonoma_county_population.htm

53. Robert Eyler, Ph.D. Economic Department Chair & Director, Center for Regional Economic Analysis

54. Sonoma State University. Report for the North Bay Leadership Council, May 24, 2007, from www.northbaycouncil.org.

55. see mission statement at www.abag.ca.gov

56. Dick Spotswood, "Local leaders fearful of regional housing goals," *MARIN INDEPENDENT JOURNAL*, June 21, 2009

57. Office of Advance Planning, 2009 "Annual Review 2008, Santa Rosa 2020: General Plan, Growth Management Ordinance, Housing Allocation Plan Ordinance," City of Santa Rosa, March 17, 2009

58. Office of Advanced Planning (2009)

59. Chris Coursey, "Growth Control, but not Growth Management," *The Press Democrat,* March 17, 2006

60. Mike McCoy, "Mayor: More rail in state's future," *The Press Democrat*, October 6, 2007

61. Willard Richards, January 2010 letter to SCTA/RCPA Board and Staff

62. see northbayecoworkforce.shutterfly.com/ and www.capsonoma.org/youthbuild.htm

63. See the US Department of Energy website and entries on its Solar American Cities program: http://www.solaramericacities.energy.gov/

64. Santa Rosa Utilities Department, Water Supply Assessment

65. Chris Coursey, "Asking a few questions about conservation," *The Press Democrat,* July 16, 2007

66. See the Foundation's website: www.lagunafoundation.org

67. See http://smartercities.nrdc.org/rankings/medium

68. from www.businessdictionary.com

69. Moody's Economy.com, "Looking for a Bottom: Considering Economic Recovery in Sonoma Count," report prepared for the Sonoma County Economic Development Board, June 2009

70. ABAG, "ABAG's 26th Annual Bay Area Economic Outlook," posted January 29th, 2010 at http://www.abag.ca.gov/cgi-bin/ newspro/viewnews.cgi?newsid1264804379,49217, 0110 rpt

71. Sonoma County Economic Development Board, *Indicators 2010,* January 2010. See also information on www.sonomaedb. org

72. Christopher Thornberg, "What's Next?," presentation sponsored by the Sonoma County Economic Development Board Foundation, Santa Rosa October 9, 2009, also posted on http://www.sonoma-county.org/edb/reports.htm

73. Robert Digitale, "Nearly I in 3 Sonoma County Homeowners Under Water," *The Press Democrat,* February 23, 2010

74. Santa Rosa Economic Sustainability Strategy document, April 2008, updated December 2009. See http://ci.santa-rosa.ca.us/ DEPARTMENTS/ECONOMICDEV/ECONDEVELOP/ Pages/default.aspx

75. see Department of Economic Development and Housing page links on the City website www.srcity.org

76. Jeff Quackenbush, "Appellate Court upholds 'Gateways' redevelopment approval," *North Bay Business Journal,* July 28, 2009

77. see www.Sonoma-county.org/edb

78. Mike McCoy, "More bad budget news for Santa Rosa," *The Press Democrat,* September 5, 2009

79. This chapter draws heavily from the reports and practices of cities which have given high priority to social sustainability with community engagement, in particular Boulder, Portland and Seattle. Thematic discussion here is especially influenced by Boulder's excellent website material at http://www. bouldercolorado.gov/ including the reports on the work that led to its Social Sustainabilty Strategic Plan, adopted in May 2007 and now being implemented. The Chapter is also greatly influenced by similar work that has been done to explore and promote social sustainability in places like Vancouver, BC, Canada and Western Australia.

80. Robert Dahlstet, "GUEST OPINION: Biggest challenge facing SR schools is not the budget," *Press Democrat,* November 25, 2009

81. Boulder, CO, Social Sustainabilty Strategic Plan

82. Listening For a Change, *We Listen*, report issued January 25, 2009, available at www.listeningforachange.org/welisten.html

83. Greg Retsinas, "An editor's message about those online comments," *The Press Democrat,* I February 10, 2010 from www.thepressdemocrat.com

84. see www.hcc-sc.org/

85. see Gaye Lebaron and Joann Mitchell (1993)

86. Robert Digitalem, "Sonoma County home prices rise; inventory dwindles." *The Press Democrat,* January 12, 2010

87. Michael Coit, "Housing affordability rises in Sonoma County," *The Press Democrat,* May 14, 2009

88. see http://www.well-beingindex.com/

89. Harvey Molotch, 1999, "Growth Machine Links, Up Down and Across," in *The Urban Growth Machine: Critical Perspectives Two Decades Later,* edited by Andrew E.G. Jonas and David Wilson, Albany, State University of New York Press

90. Richard Gendron and G. William Donhoff, 2009, *The Leftmost City,* Boulder: Westview Press

INDEX